Radicals in
social work

Radical Social Policy

GENERAL EDITOR

Vic George

*Professor of Social Policy and
Administration and Social Work
University of Kent*

Radicals in social work

Daphne Statham

Routledge & Kegan Paul
London, Henley and Boston

First published in 1978
by Routledge & Kegan Paul Ltd
39 Store Street
London WC1E 7DD
Broadway House,
Newtown Road,
Henley-on-Thames,
Oxon RG9 1EN and
9 Park Street
Boston, Mass. 02108, USA
Set in IBM Press Roman by
Pentagon Printing Group
Soho Square, London W1
and printed in Great Britain by
Lowe & Brydone Ltd
ISBN 0 7100 8801 9 (c)
ISBN 0 7100 8802 7 (p)

CONTENTS

To the younger generation who have already turned us into liberals

Acknowledgments

Acknowledgments are due to students, colleagues and friends who, through discussing their ideas with me, have helped me to develop my own thinking, and to Jim, Eleanor and Tom who, because we live together, have contributed much more than ideas.

Introduction

This is not a book about methods, but an attempt to examine how the analyses of the liberation movements affect some of the theory underpinning social work. It is based on a conviction that the substitution of one method for another — for instance, community work or integrated methods for casework — carries in itself no radical implications unless accompanied by changes in theory. The main objective is not to formulate answers, but rather to offer a starting point for discussion for students seeking to challenge the socio-economic base of society, and hence traditional theories. Whether the ideas expressed here are accepted, reformulated or rejected is less important than that the debate continues.

It will become clear that much of the subject-matter can be used by liberal radicals, that is those seeking change within the context of the existing socio-economic order. This is because the assumption has been made that in the UK social work operates within and not apart from capitalism. As institutionalised social work cannot have a revolutionary function, and, irrespective of their origin, ideas taken into it have to become liberalised — divested of their revolutionary impetus. Except in the liberal sense, therefore, the term 'radical social work' is a contradiction. For those seeking to work towards an alternative society, their main base is in movements outside, not inside, social work.

In spite of these limitations, the argument is that there is an onus on the left-wing social worker to try to ensure that the analysis of movements in the wider society has an impact on theory and practice. While it is important to be clear that intervention will focus on effects, not causes, small moves can have beneficial effects on the lives of people now and this generation should not be mortgaged for some future utopian ideal. An alternative society will not miraculously emerge; it has to be worked towards on a number of levels and in a number of ways. Moves have to be made from analysis to action which is appropriate in the current situation, and the objective is to distinguish between what can be done and what must wait until later, what can be drawn into social work and what must be located elsewhere.

This is no small task. Change is inherent in capitalism; cultural and ideological changes are already occurring which are not radical in their import, and these are affecting the disciplines from which social work has traditionally taken and adapted its theory. They are indications of responsiveness, not of an alteration in direction. In the process of selecting and integrating theories from other disciplines — sometimes called electic teaching — consensus often appears to exist whereas in fact there is controversy and doubt. The dynamic of these disciplines needs to be drawn into social work teaching for both the left winger and the liberal. This can only be accomplished by groups of people with a common ideological framework and area of experience who have betweeen them a detailed knowledge of each of the contributing disciplines. A book by an individual is no substitute for this collective and continuing task.

The choice of the areas covered in this book was not arbitrary. It arose from a conviction that theoretical proficiency is not in itself sufficient; theory has to be based in experience. If we are not black, although we may participate in action, we cannot contribute to the *analysis* of black oppression, because, however enlightened our views are thought to be, the white are among the oppressors. Like any other persons, social workers are vulnerable to paternalistic and elitist tendencies; professionalism is but a thin, protective veneer. A deliberate decision was, therefore, made to limit discussion to those subjects where my experience as a person and as a member of different collectives could be combined with an understanding of theory. Obviously such a book is incomplete and the topics covered may lack logical sequence for the reader, but learning is not a neat process of setting one block upon another. It is patchy and there is frequently a need to demolish in order to rebuild.

My debt to the women's liberation movement will be obvious, but I must acknowledge the contribution made to my thinking by one group, Mothers in Action; from them I have learnt the most and been the closest. I should also make it clear that the views expressed in the book are entirely personal, and in no way represent those of the council for which I work. Finally, it is important to recognise that because of the very nature of radicalism this book will hopefully be out of date by the time it is published.

1

Radicalism and social work

Introduction

The predilection for discussing social work in Britain in isolation
from its social context is evidenced in the interpretation of the current
interest in social action and reform as a new phenomenon called
'radical social work'. Boundary alterations, which are occurring
simultaneously elsewhere in society, are mistaken for indicators of
fundamental changes within the profession. Throughout most of its
history social work has to a greater or lesser extent subscribed to a
liberal radical tradition.[1] Given the structure of British social work,
more is not possible, and it cannot be regarded as a vehicle for
revolution. This is not an argument for left-wing radicals to get out,
or keep out, of social work; they face the problem of living and
working within capitalism in every situation. The need is rather to
analyse the nature of the problems encountered in order to identify
where there is room for movement in social work and where action
has to be located outside it.

The liberal radical tradition

Though the form is specific to a historical period, liberal radicalism is
part of the structure of the professions, and it is no particular merit
of social work that it exists within it. The present search for radical
alternatives[2] is not peculiar to social work, it is also in evidence in
education, medicine and the law. Neither the apparent previous

absence of radicalism nor the current efforts of the professional
association to legitimise a new form of liberal radicalism[3] can be
explained by peering into the entrails of social work. The search has
to be located in the context of the wider society. Conclusions such as
John Cypher's that it was the numerical predominance of women and
their 'feminine' traits of passivity and nurturance which prevented the
development of action and conflict orientations[4] are quickly shown to
be irrelevant when, removed from its splendid isolation, the record of
social work is compared with male dominated professions whose lack
of radicalism is no less marked. In the contemporary situation there is
a general acceptance that the socio-economic structure has failed to
achieve its objectives, and tradition-oriented groups are re-assessing
their position and casting around for means which will more
successfully work towards their aims. Within their own philosophy
these solutions can often be called radical. Indeed the term 'radical
right' has become acceptable.

Changes which occur within the liberal tradition to which social
work subscribes present no basic threat to British society because,
whatever the theory used, there is an acceptance of a dynamic. The
rules, or some of the rules, of any society have to be altered from time
to time to take the effects of change into account. Points requiring
minor or even major adjustment need to be identified and new solutions
tested. This is one of the functions of liberal radicalism. Changes in
social policy demanded by the liberal may be ahead of the time in
which they are thought to be politically practical, but frequently, even
in the early stages, they are seen as being 'right in principle'. These
advocates of reform often move within their own life-time from being
regarded as radicals to receiving social recognition and acclamation.
Such is the fate and fame of those who campaigned for universal
education, the old-age pension, the health service. While it is often
necessary to contain the liberals' enthusiasm for their cause, they are
not rejected, because they do not challenge the basis of society.
Whatever the label attached — the mixed economy, welfare
capitalism or state capitalism — it remains the same and the prime
goal is profit in a class society. Although a certain amount of conflict
is becoming acceptable in the pursuit of a better deal,[5] in the main
liberal radicals work within the rules or seek to change them by
legitimate means. They like to be identified with a principle of justice
and right dealing[6] not with a class or party. Within this tradition the
polarisation of care and social change with social control functions
are misconceptions because each function is dependent on the
existence of the other; they are not opposites, but different sides
of the same coin.

Left radicalism

Left radicalism, in contrast, challenges the basis of the institution, the ideology, and in the long term works for a new and not a changed society. The analysis has its base in a different political theory and affects not the parts but the whole. This distinction holds whether attention is directed towards the social and the economic structure or towards personal relationships. Marxist political theory is most highly developed in the first area and the problems created by the absence of an adequate theory in the second have been recognised. Like Reich in the 1920s, the radical left is trying to develop a theory of personality which is consistent with socialism. Currently, part of the debate is centred around whether or not Freudian theory offers a base from which it can be developed,[7] but there is little doubt that whatever the validity of the original theory, Freud's ideas have been used by those who refer to them as a constraining and not a liberating force.[8] Left-wing radicals, it should be made clear, have not turned their interest to social work. The focus on personality and emotional experience has quite separate origins, in the recognition by the young of the need to challenge a culture which values the intellective and devalues the non-intellective powers of the human personality.[9]

To counter a world based on reason, objective reality and knowledge, a politics of experience has emerged which sees experience, complete with all its emotions, as a source of theory.[10] Experience is sought in the non-intellective areas to find personhood and a life-style that rejects a technologically based culture. In order to structure accumulated experience and develop it further, some have turned towards oriental philosophers and others to psychoanalytic theories.[11] They have looked to areas, and, in the latter instance, to theories which are the concern of social work. These movements have produced reactions in traditional circles and it is now not uncommon to hear the failure of technological solutions discussed in a variety of contexts.[12] Ironically, in this same period social work was increasingly lamenting the 'psychoanalytic deluge' and seeking influence in setting up social programmes and in social organisation. Some social workers will participate in the development of theory based in experience through participation in groups outside the profession, but all need to be aware that the questions being asked call into dispute theories and principles which have been traditionally regarded as basic to social work.

Radical doubt

Erich Fromm describes radicalism as 'not primarily a set of ideas but an approach, an attitude characterised by the motto "de omnibus dubitatum" '. He uses the word 'doubt' not to describe an inability to decide or to be committed, but as the readiness and capacity for critical questioning of all assumptions and institutions which have become idols under the same common sense, logic or what is supposed to be "natural" '. Radical doubt is 'dialectical in as much as it comprehends the unfolding of oppositions and aims at a new synthesis which negates and affirms'.[13]

The danger lies not simply in the identification of negatives in an existing situation, but comes from two other sources. First, there is the intention to seek alternatives, and second, the conviction that these must emerge from people with direct experience and not from an analysis made by outsiders. Inherent in this idea is a belief in the capacity of people to work towards understanding their situation and to find ways to change it. That this process begins by focusing on local issues is not a major stumbling block because, as Illich points out in relation to education, it is necessary for only one idol to topple and others will follow.[14] The approach is always subversive, but not invariably revolutionary.[15] For left-wing radicals, however, the primary purpose would be to work towards a change in the economic base and underlying their radical doubt is a political theory. On a theoretical level left-wing radicalism is attractive to many intellectuals, but applied in practice, in whatever field or group, it provokes extreme reactions. Social workers can expect no better treatment than anyone else — no appeal can be made to whatever rules are thought to exist, since the objective is to change the game.

Who is a social worker?

Before examining radicalism within social work it is necessary to identify how the terms 'social work' and 'social worker' are being used. 'Social worker' is used to apply to a person designated as such by the agency in which he or she is working in the day-care, field or residential setting. Whether or not community work is part of social work is under debate. Although it is clear that social work theories have a relevance to community work, and vice versa, there is at present no consensus about its position and it is not intended to anticipate the outcome here by proclaiming one way or the other.

Quite apart from arguments about the merits of professionalism and whether social work belongs to a profession or semi-profession, definitions which limit the use of the term 'social worker' to the qualified are misleading when less than 40 per cent of those in practice fall into this category.[16] Often a restrictive use of the term seems to be part of an attempt to create unity in the face of the diversity of skills and functions which are required to maintain social work in agencies, whether statutory or voluntary. The tendency to stress unity is shared by other professional and semi-professional groups who also emphasise consensus and congruence to maximise the promotion of their self-interests, and in the interests of stability, rather than recognising and using conflict and divergence to promote change. The effects of this process on social work education are commented on by Bender and Clark. In their words, 'harmony of means and goals between professional aspirants and their mentors under changing and volatile social conditions is dysfunctional to the development of militant attributes and assertive behaviour,' which are required in the struggle to legitimate the right to perform new roles.[17]

The context of social work

Whilst it may be important for social work to try to order its own house, it is equally vital to avoid descriptions which, because they ignore the societal context of social work,[18] are irrelevant to those outside and in particular those who experience it. Although belonging to a group of 'helping professions' with its hallmark described as 'the desire and ability to proffer help to clients',[19] social work is not 'unambiguously helper' nor is the relationship offered unlimited.[20] There is a gentle, almost imperceptible slide from principles and theories designed to operate in private psychoanalytic practice to social work whose locus of activity is mainly in large, bureaucratically organised agencies with boundaries set by statute. In addition, these agencies frequently do not have exclusive responsibility for their clients' treatment plans. Although the relationships between them are not always clearly defined, the responsibility is often shared with other organisations, some at least of which accept their function as being primarily that of exercising social control.

The social worker is not operating in a simple model of private paying patient and analyst whose concern is the unconscious. However much individual style differentiates one social worker from another,[21] they are not freelance. These points have been re-iterated by many writers, but seem to have little effect on the way social work is viewed by many within it. For instance, the contract is sometimes seen as a new way to offer clients an open and equal relationship, but the basis of social worker–client relations can be changed without either of them consenting. Not only is the power between them uneven, but intervention from outside the relationship and the agency cannot be prevented. Contracts cannot be made in any honesty between worker and client in voluntary or statutory agency because, in respect of the former, the contractor in the first instance is the agency and, in the second, the state. If it is claimed that the contract simply means that both client and worker should be clear about the task they are undertaking, and the limits imposed on them, it is surely unnecessary to import semi-legal terminology to describe what used to be regarded as basic to good practice. More often the idea seems to be seen as creating a better status for the client. In this aim it is reminiscent of nineteenth-century labour law which proposed that a contract between an individual employee and employer was free and equal.[22] The trade union movement have fought this idea, and social work would do well to look to labour history before proceeding further along this path as a means of improving the status of clients.[23]

Social work is part of welfare

A corollary of the failure to take into account the impact of the societal structure is the extraction of social work from the total welfare system. The current interest in developing links between groups whose work impinges on social work is a tacit recognition of the convergence of a number of parts in work with clients. In many instances the distinctive feature is not the presence or absence of other agencies in addition to a social worker, but the specific combination of the workers involved — the health visitor, the doctor, the police, the supplementary benefits officer. Each has to satisfy their own area of responsibility and accountability and at the same time co-operate with each other because overlap is inevitable. Although the combination will differ with the nature of the intervention, the inter-connectedness is established by the structure of welfare and affects social workers in both voluntary and statutory agencies. The point of entry into the welfare system is often not significant to the client in the long term. For instance, those receiving supplementary benefit often find that this brings a social worker in its train.[24] The situation can be experienced differently by clients and social workers. For the professional there is the recognition of the connectedness of social work with that of others and an emphasis on developing inter-professional or inter-agency perspectives, an approach compatible with systems analysis and undoubtedly helpful to some clients. On the other hand, among others, their awareness of the inevitable connections between social work and other parts of the welfare system brings with it a realisation that the weight given to the client's perceptions is frequently small. Moreover, within the majority of social work agencies the client has no control over to whom information is passed, and, irrespective of guidelines about confidentiality, many clients are not informed about who knows what, least of all consulted before information is passed on. These clients see little potential in working with social workers to improve their position, but seek instead to establish groups outside which can act upon it.

The failure to locate social work in the total context of welfare, and to locate welfare in the social context, has serious implications for clients. Bitensky illustrates this point by the case of a client whose welfare assistance was withdrawn because he refused home visits from a caseworker. Although the case went to a US District Court and subsequently to the Supreme Court the social work profession remained silent on the issue of the client's rights. This was left to the lawyers. He concludes that the absence of a societal perspective meant that 'the profession was unable to discern that to take away a welfare client's dignity as an American citizen vitiated the very rehabilitative process it was trying to further'[25] The example is American and the situation cannot be directly replicated here, but there are unnervingly close comparisons. Many clients think one already exists in the operation of Section I of the 1963 Children's Act, where there is no opportunity for appeal against a decision and no reasons need be given. Frequently, help given under this section is conditional on a social worker being allocated. There is for some an unenviable choice between a loss of available, needed resources and becoming a client irrespective of the origin of the need. Help is conditional. The pattern of tell-me-your-problem, or, alternatively, behave-well-and-I-will-give-you-material-help, is by no means extinct in practice.

Simple models which extract social work from its societal context may have a limited use, but they are extremely dangerous when transferred to practice situations without an acute sense that a model is useful only in so far as there is an awareness of what is omitted from it, and moves from the micro- to the macro-social situation and vice versa are identified. Failing this, the tendency is to polarise social work with welfare and service provision, environmental work with relationship work, the individual with the collective[26] In spite of the currency of ideas about generic and systems theory, these oppositions are retained and one approach is often seen as inherently superior to another. Workers within the same agency or community can find themselves divided according to the particular focus of their work and the status allocated to it. This not only weakens social work, but also blocks attempts to develop a coherent framework which takes into account that the important factor for the client, group or community is the relevance of what is offered to their particular situation. The residential and day service worker are frequently more important in the lives of clients than the field worker whose status and pay is higher and whose training opportunities have been far greater. Polarisation prevents both joint analysis and action — it is a simplistic tool functioning through the creation of oppositions; no interaction or synthesis is possible.

Welfare, and hence social work, has a societal function. Welfare capitalism is used to describe the contemporary phase in its development.[27] It is true that Marx saw welfare provision as the concessions wrestled by the working class, and that to describe social work simply as the creature of capitalism is too crude.[28] But it is equally misleading to see social work in isolation from the social and economic structure in which it operates, or to fail to identify the specific patterning and the degree of state involvement in social work practice and education. Sources of state involvement vary, but there is evidence that, compared with some countries, state involvement in Britain is comparatively high. There is financial support for social work agencies and indirectly for social work education, and the boundaries of much of the profession's work are made and changed by statute and statutory regulations.[29] Direct comparisons between countries about the potential for radical action or alignments with clients are misleading if they do not take into account differences in the nature of state involvement with social work, and hence the expectations of it.

Political context and history

In order to analyse the specific characteristics and functions of social work, the historical and political context have to be taken into account. What is possible in post-revolutionary China cannot be directly transferred to the British scene. Within the same country context remains vital. Marxist and post-Allende Chile expect different things from social workers. Under Allende consciousness-raising was recognised as a professional activity, under the Generals it is accompanied by imprisonment. There was a change from consciousness-raising being a legitimate activity for social workers to its being defined as a politically subversive individual or group act. After the revolution social work may well become revolutionary, but it does not and cannot initiate one itself. The fact of being, or the act of seeking to become, a profession implies legitimation by the existing society and in consequence no profession can have a revolutionary function.[30] For many left-wing radicals the absence of a profession with its claim to autonomy would be regarded as one of the signs of a post-revolutionary situation, or would at least be one of the things to work towards. It is not that skills in relationships would no longer be required, or that social change would no longer be necessary, but that those who have, or acquire, these skills would be accountable to the community and not to a group which seeks both power and privilege for itself. The aim would be to extend the welfare state so that it is controlled and organised by the people who use it.[31]

This is far removed from ideas about advocacy, welfare rights or the social worker as broker. This terminology does not challenge a concept of welfare in which there are givers and receivers. The basis for the control of knowledge and resources, the right to define problems and suggest solutions, remains with social workers and other legitimised experts. For instance, writing on the social worker as broker, Hunter states:

> Few other groups have such natural opportunities to move around among different sectors of the community, understand the views and requirements of different groups, to know what is going on here and what is going on there, and to assess individual and group capacities to accomplish specific goals.[32]

Here the social worker stands in a central and powerful position. The problem of conflicting demands and loyalties created by the various sources of its legitimacy and authority[33] is resolved by placing social work above them all like a kind of arbitration tribunal for society. In contrast, citizens' rights is an attempt to move both the knowledge and the skills from the remit of welfare workers to more popularly based groups. Ultimately this knowledge would be part of basic education.[34] This in no way denies that social workers need to know about their clients' rights, but asserts that in the long term this knowledge belongs to all citizens and the skills of advocacy should not be contained within social work, the law or any other professional group. It is an aspect of a much wider argument about the redistribution of power, whether in terms of knowledge, skills or access to resources, from specific legitimated groups. The task of identifying how the skills acquired by social workers can be used in bringing about this process and maintaining its momentum has scarcely been embarked upon.

Social work as a reactive profession

There are individual social workers who are radical in both the liberal or left-wing sense, but to claim that the profession stands as a kind of advance humanitarian guard between the individual and technological change[35] is a good intention which ignores social work's position as a reactive institution. It follows and responds rather than leads.[36] This is in accord with Meyer's view that the viability of social work rests in its ability to accommodate to changing perceptions[37] The question of whose perception is pertinent. BASW sees social workers deriving their legitimacy and right to practice from the community, the clients, the law and the agency,[38] but accommodation to the perceptions of clients cannot be so great that they deviate far from the norms of a specific society. It is part of the function of the ideology inherent in theory to prevent this happening and the law in certain aspects reinforces the limits. While the social work profession may try to influence the making of the law relating to its practice, it would be quite wrong to assume that there is unity or even a majority agreement among its ranks about what, in specific instances, their recommendations should be. Nor is there any sign that they are powerful enough to act as an effective pressure group when significant shifts are taking place in social policy[39]

Through the analysis of the interaction between the political system of America and changes in social work theory, Bitensky offers a useful corrective to the more frequent assumption that developments in social work are solely a reflection of growth and changes in its own theory base and in the acquisition of neutral knowledge. He argues that the theories and values of social work inevitably interact with the political system. The cumulative result of this interaction is such that, without a clear understanding of the process, 'the profession may find itself in the position of forwarding alien political objectives under the impression that these goals are congruent with the needs of clients and the values of the profession'.[40] The Mental Patients Union and the Claimants' Union, who both claim the right to make their own analysis and to define needs and solutions, appear to have decided that social work in Britain is already in the position described by Bitensky.[41]

Client control or client participation

Because the ultimate aim is the extension of the welfare state so that it is controlled by those who use it, it is logical that client control over welfare institutions is a goal for the left-wing radical. At this point the term 'client' would become meaningless. In the meantime, the issue is whether or not client participation is useful in working towards this end. What is and is not the client's business is a relatively untouched issue beyond the boundaries of the client's or a group's own case. Ginsberg thinks that social workers will have to accept a change and that who is appointed to the staff of an agency, for instance, is the client's business. 'We shall have to develop an approach which recognises that our consumers are going to have a much greater control of the services themselves and a much greater share in making the decisions.' Whether or not the clients are 'ready' is not the question to be asked; mistakes, he says, will be made, and social workers will have to live with them.[42] This is much the same for clients who now have to live with the swings in fashion, differences in policy and provision from one agency and one area to another. The inclusion of clients on social service department committees was suggested in the Seebohm Report,[43] but it seems not to be taken with much seriousness by the majority of agencies, although some voluntary organisations have made, or are beginning to make, moves towards this end. It is doubtful whether one or two individual clients can make much of an impact on the policies of large, hierarchical agencies. Even with the backing of a collective support group the task is an uphill one. There may be room for movement, or membership may be token and of more use to the agency than to the group, so that involvement is refused because energies are most effectively directed towards the development of alternative services.

In the majority of social work agencies, with no client participation and no client influence over appointments or the formulation of policy, a clear distinction between the social worker and the client is crucial. Irrespective of the individual social worker's standpoint, it is not unity of purpose that needs stressing, but a recognition of actual and potential divergence that is vital. With social work's adherence to the position of the 'unambiguous helper', the identification of points at which it and the services it offers are not helpful become problematic. George and Wilding have identified how this operated in contacts with motherless families:

> Social workers had to ration scarce resources . . . are forced to act as protectors and guardians of inadequate services. Their professional skills, that enabled them to handle dissatisfied clients with tact and understanding, may reduce public pressures for the improvement of social services. In this respect they unwittingly act against the improvement of the very social services they administer.[44]

Similarly, within the present structure, individual clients on agency committees can become absorbed in resolving problems as they are at present defined, and lose the impetus of their own analysis and its logic for action. In the majority of cases at this point in time clients will probably fare better in organisations from which they can act upon social work.

Collective support groups

Many of these groups will not be radical in their politics and their overall political position will be liberal and not left. It is misleading to view radicalism as all-pervasive either in persons or groups. Women's liberationists have given numerous examples of the left's behaviour towards women which originates from their being men in a male-dominated society and not from political analysis[45] The other liberation movements could add their own examples of similar inconsistencies. Analysis based in experience and the demand for access to resources on the basis of need, not income and status, is a socialist principle, but the use of that principle by some collective action and support groups does not mean that they are advocating a socialist society. Their analysis and demands are frequently specific to their group. Because their radicalism is specific and encapsulated, it is possible for them to contain a wide range of political views. They ask only for a better deal and more freedom for themselves, which, though necessitating reforms, is not intended to alter the economic and social structure of society. Although the potential of these groups should not be under-estimated, they are in contrast with those which, while asking for present reform, see liberation as being possible only within the framework of a socialist society. These, therefore, move from their own experience to express solidarity with other collective support groups and in addition with socialist movements. They see their strength in solidarity, not in isolation and competition for scarce resources.

It has been reported that radicalism in social workers increased with the amount of training they received,[46] but this sort of radicalism is rarely politicised and it does not invariably link with movements in the wider society — to do so is seen by some as unprofessional.[47] The danger in the separation is that it frequently leads to proposals for reforms, models of behaviour which ignore experience. Comprehensive reforms suggested by researchers are rarely, if ever, implemented in full, and piecemeal reforms make little impact on situations, although they retain an importance as symbols of humanitarian concern. In addition, preventative programmes ignore structural and class issues which work to minimise their effect or simply to transfer the stress from one area or group to another. In the end the only resource social work is left with is the idea from which the suggested reforms originated.'The good parent', 'children's rights', these ideas are applied to the lives of children and their parents without the provision of the basic resources and serve only to measure the distance between the social worker's expectations and the parent's situation; between what they would like to, or feel they should do, and what is possible in the absence of resources or support. Ideas become moral exhortations emptied of content or possibility, except for those who are already privileged.

The left-wing radical in social work

The nature and function of social work requires the left-wing radical to be constantly stepping outside. The step back in again is made in attempting to make an impact on theory and practice as a result of an analysis of the experience required. The radical's theory and practice is always in a process of becoming because account has to be taken of the reactions it provokes.[48] Reactions are not always in terms of head-on collisions. Marcuse stands alongside others when he comments 'that every thing in this society can be co-opted, every thing digested'.[49] Within social work, left-wing radicalism can be talked about with some degree of impunity, but its practice is strictly circumscribed. In action it is often identified less by overt characteristics than by the political views of those involved, and frequently appears to be more like liberal radicalism than different from it. For the liberal radical, however, the change sought is limited and is an end in itself — 'the target of change . . . is those policies of institutions in our society which cause problems to the clients of social workers'[50] — for the other these objectives are tactics which form part of a longer-term struggle.

Those who decide to remain in traditional social work or on its fringes know that compromise, not purity, is the rule. Asking for political consistency between the private and work world is to seek a position of privilege denied to the majority of people in British society, and in particular to those clients whose private lives become a public work world for the social worker, irrespective of the political views of the latter. It is true that the separation of the world of work from the personal was a prerequisite of rapid industrialisation, and that this is validated in liberal philosophy which sees true freedom existing in individual castles. Analysis, however, identifies the nature of the beast; action has to take into account both the political situation and our own involvement with it as well as the advantages social workers receive by virtue of their position.

To seek and acquire a high degree of purity and consistency is to have achieved a position of privilege. For the majority, an active and open search leads either to a withdrawal from action or an ejection from it. To drop out by choice is an act which, as the term implies, assumes that the person has been on the inside,[51] and for many who tire of its pleasures the journey in again is relatively simple. To drop out

13

in comfort depends on the possession of, or access to, capital which is unavailable to the working class who may be equally keen to sample the pleasures of rural life or to seek the exploration of the self, but the options are not open to them.[32] An editorial in 'Case Con' makes a similar point when it states that:

> you cannot escape the contradictions inherent in capitalism simply by being unemployed, or in our case working outside the State Social Service network. The inevitable word of caution — it is a delusion to pretend that we can ignore the limitations and constraints placed upon us.[53]

Radicalism may well need its occasional rebels who become martyrs for a cause, but there is a danger that the only positive contribution they make is the temporary moral boost for the individual or group concerned. George Jackson's Soledad letters make a clear distinction between futile acts of rebellion originating from outbursts of anger and the acts of a disciplined revolutionary.[54] 'Case Con' also refers to the 'sacked worker, naked and isolated [who] contributes little to radical ideas or socialist strategy'.[55] The significance of the rebel is to be measured in terms of the function he or she serves in relation to goals in the shorter and longer term. Neither activism nor verbalism should be confused with revolutionary work, which relies on discipline and action being taken after analysis based on reflection.[56]

Degrees of radicalism cannot be determined by crude measures of whether a person is inside or outside traditional social work, working within the liberal tradition or outside it. The game of 'lefter than thou' is particularly useless in situations which require action. Its players may have been oppressed, but the oppression has mainly been in the mind.[57] They are comparable to Paulo Friere's category of reflection which has sacrificed action[58] — the armchair revolutionary. The problem is to identify the nature of the task and the type of activity that is appropriate in the current political situation. It is equally vital to distinguish between an individual's disappointment either with the effect or extent of his or her own contribution, or personal impatience aroused by the slow pace of change, and the long-term struggle which must be seen in collective terms.

David Cooper's idea of 'urban guerrilla welfare' is worth exploring by those faced with the problem of living and working with capitalism. The urban guerrilla 'achieves a solidarity with the people that aims not only at their future liberation but at a very present accompaniment for them in their very present travail'.[59] He sees them operating as lawyers, doctors, guardians of the people's courts and prisons. The political situation in Argentina where Cooper was writing involved the accompaniment of guerrilla warfare, but the idea is useful in the first world context in identifying a locus of commitment and the nature of the activity. In an earlier book he made a clear distinction between activities that are relevant and possible in a pre-revolutionary, as opposed to a revolutionary, society. 'What we have to do in this first world context is to accumulate experience in the pre-revolutionary situation that can only achieve full social expression after the revolution.' He concedes that there is no way around the fact that people need money in order to live, but thinks that the development of the cell — the micro-political experience — is strategic in official institutions, and outside them.[60]

Consciousness-raising and social work

Consciousness-raising is an activity taking place within the cell and is the process by which experience becomes translated from a collection of individual descriptions into political awareness — the personal becomes politicised. Because some social workers see the incorporation of these activities into social work practice as a desirable activity and a possible goal, the relationship between social work and consciousness-raising needs exploration. The most publicised literature, that of Friere and Illich,[61] quickly reveal similarities between them, but it is misleading to confuse the presence of common elements with overall objectives. When the two wholes, as opposed to their parts, are compared, the differences emerging are enormous.

Similarities are easily identified. First, in general terms consciousness-raising attempts to awaken people's awareness in order that they can critically reflect on their experience, and, as a result of this process, take action. This can be compared with social work's aim of enhancing a person's, a group's, or a community's capacity to look at their own situation, their own part in it, to assess it, to make connections between causes and consequences and to take appropriate action. Secondly, both are based on a belief in the capacity of people, usually devalued by the society in which they live, to undertake these activities and to have a greater control over their lives. Thirdly, both subscribe to the value of creating opportunities to speak about the unspoken, that is those experiences and feelings which were thought to be peculiar to oneself. Fourth, social group work and consciousness-raising values the expression of the previously unspoken in a group situation. The common ground, however, rapidly disappears. Consciousness-raising is at least politically subversive, if not always revolutionary, in intent.[62] The relationship it seeks to explore is that between people and the structure of the society in which they live — between rich and poor, black and white, men and women, adults and children, the powerful and the powerless. The awareness it seeks to create is of cultural myths which support the retention of a specific patterning of these relationships, and of one's own conditioning. Consciousness-raising, therefore, moves from the experience of the individual, to the group, to the whole of society.[63] The function of social work in Great Britain, which has sought professional status and been awarded considerable statutory powers and responsibilities, is quite different. At the most it has a developmental or systematic change function.[64] That this at times necessitates political action and challenges to established policy does not translate social work from its liberal radical tradition into a revolutionary dimension, nor can activities which have revolutionary objectives be absorbed into it without changing their essential nature.

Social worker activity, as opposed to statements of intent, focuses on specific situations, irrespective of whether individuals, groups or communities are involved. Boundaries are set around the situation and the frames of reference used are all consistent with developmental change within the existing framework of society. Action planned must be 'appropriate' or 'realistic' and the definition of these terms clearly indicates an acceptance of the status quo, not as a tactic for the present context, but as a continuing feature. It follows that although the term 'consciousness-raising' has been incorporated into social work jargon in America as an alternative, more fashionable term than social group work, the essential move from the group to the whole of society has to be omitted, or the relationship explored is essentially consistent with social work's developmental function. In one instance the term was used to describe a group looking at the problem created for obese women in contemporary society.[65] What emerges is a therapeutic experience for the members and sometimes the identification of the need for adaptations. This is not to under-estimate the significance of the experience or of changes achieved, but seeks rather to clarify that the nature of the objectives are quite different from consciousness-raising in the political sense.

Rather than being drawn by attractive ideas emerging largely from the third world and from revolutionary situations where social work has done no more than react to politically initiated changes, left-wing radicals in the British context have to analyse what is possible in the here and now. The action takes place in the first world, and people, including Friere, who try to implement ideas based on consciousness-raising in traditional, conservative societies are removed from them. Finally, the argument that a major part, if not all of, consciousness-raising activities must remain outside social work in the current British context is more complex than an awareness of the restraints imposed on radical social workers. It is clear from writers like Friere and Illich that consciousness-raising cannot be undertaken on a group's, or someone's, behalf,[66] or by a person seeking either to retain his or her status as a professional or as an elitist radical. The assumption is that there is a fundamental difference between 'the kind of knowledge which may be acquired by a subject who contemplates an object that is separate from himself – an object placed, as it were, at a distance from himself' and that acquired by living in and experiencing the situation.[67] This view originally referred to the development of class consciousness, but it has been applied to other oppressed groups in the first and third world context, and rejects the professional approach with its reliance on objective, not subjective, definitions of reality and knowledge. Although there is a slight shift in social work towards accommodating this trend in the search for the 'consumer's viewpoint', there remains a basic assumption that knowledge is a neutral commodity. It is claimed that social work holds an uncommitted position and is concerned 'with individuals and groups in their social situation, not with abstractions such as the system or humanity in the mass, not with politics or ideologies'.[68] The assertion of consciousness-raising is that there can be no understanding without a theory based in direct experience. It is important not to confuse this approach with a rejection of knowledge as such. The debate is about who frames the questions, and whose version of reality or reasonableness is accorded status, and who must undertake the work analysis.

The message from Friere, Illich and others is quite clear as these quotations show: 'the pedagogy of the oppressed cannot be developed or practised by the oppressors'[69] (Illich); 'Blacks are and must be the primary soldiers in the war against racism. Outsiders do not and cannot fight a war for insiders without transforming the fight into a battle for something else, which whatever its own intrinsic merits is inevitably more or less irrelevant to the original group's cause'[70] (Lerner). The examples are endless, the point is that the development of consciousness, to be successful in overcoming the barriers set up in the mind by culture and ideology, must involve work for groups and individuals who are themselves oppressed. In the third world context the peasant's fear of the master has to be exorcised by their own action,[71] in the first world the barriers identified in the idea of relative deprivation have to be seen and overcome by those who hold them. Irrespective of claims to carry a humanitarian tradition, as institutionalised, social work is both outsider and oppressor in the specific sense.

A number of issues need, however, to be explored and tested out in practice. For instance, can the first two stages of consciousness-raising activity be moved into social work without losing the political dimension entirely or eliminating the possibility of the third and final stage being undertaken outside social work?[72] What function would the social worker have in this group? If Illich's position is taken, the contribution *qua* social worker would be minimal. If one or two of the stages can be undertaken in social work, who benefits most, the clients, the individual social worker or the profession? The left-wing radical will be primarily interested in these and related questions but issues are also raised for the liberal radical who seeks to ensure that social work continues to react and adapt to change. For instance, given the emphasis developing in the wider society on consumer participation, how can social work establish links with consciousness-raising groups as a means of obtaining information about client-defined experiences? These groups are often composed of people who could potentially become clients or who are already clients. Detailed descriptions of what it is like to be poor, black, woman, gay, offers a gauge against which traditional theories and practice guidelines can be tested. Redefinition of experience and needs also offers the possibility of bringing service provision closer to the needs of clients. In addition, in common with collective support groups, consciousness-raising activities have succeeded where social work has so often failed. They have enabled people to regain or achieve for the first time a sense of human dignity with the discovery that what has been seen as private, isolated experience with all the connotations of inadequacy, contain large areas which are shared with others in similar situations because of existing external rather than personal and internal constraints. This has for some social workers given impetus to the move towards group and community work and an increased recognition of the dangers inherent in those aspects of case work which concentrated almost exclusively on the uniquenes of human experience, as opposed to seeing this as part of a wider whole. There seem, therefore, to be a number of benefits for social work itself in moving towards extracting the non-revolutionary aspects from the analysis of consciousness-raising groups. The left-wing radical has to be careful not to mistake this process, which supports the profession's continuance, with major changes in the functions of social work in the wider society.

The options open to social workers wishing to participate in consciousness-raising activities in the full sense of the word seem to include joining a group outside social work on the basis of their personal experience, and to join or set up groups with other social workers to analyse their own positions; a more difficult task would be to test the possibilities of social workers and the clients with whom they are involved meeting together, accumulating experience and trying to learn whether and where it can be used.

Social work, liberation and the person

Although the importance is fully accepted in the short term of
identifying inconsistencies and negatives in social welfare and working
for reforms, the writer cannot follow Martin Rein in his total
identification of radical social work with social policy.[73] Leaving
aside the objection that there are economic and social factors which
prevent reform solving problems, liberation on these fronts must be
accompanied by personal liberation. David Cooper writes:

> It seems to me that a cardinal failure of all past revolutions has
> been the disassociation of liberation on the mass social level,
> i.e. liberation of whole classes in economic and political terms, and
> liberation of the individual and concrete groups in which he is
> directly engaged. If we are to talk of revolution today our talk will
> be meaningless unless we effect some union between the macro-
> social and the micro-social, between inner and outer reality.[74]

Like Wilhelm Reich earlier, he is not prepared to leave the development
of theories about people to the politically conservative.[75] A number
of radical writers agree that living through redefinition is painful and
stressful and that a companion on the journey is helpful.[76] Whoever
it is, a commitment to the possibility of redefinition through reflection
offers at least some hope that the aim is not a journey backwards in
time as an end in itself. With their knowledge of the effects of stress
and the difficulty of change, social workers could make a contribution.
Although the part they play would be small in terms of the total
task, it could in specific instances be significant.

Social workers involved in the liberation movements and collective
support groups can also assist in breaking down the massive denial of
what is different or deviant within the membership of the profession.
A recognition that all of us become old masks other areas of overlap
between the divisions of client and worker. There are numerous social
workers whose life situations conflict with what is considered to be
normal, mature, acceptable behaviour within mainstream social work
— they have had 'nervous breakdowns', are gay, are members of
broken families, are women's liberationists and therefore not
'feminine'. The liberation movements and the collective support groups
have enabled people to make an assertion of solidarity with others
who are usually on a different side of the fence. By allowing the private
to become public, the discovery is of how much there is in common and
of mutual support, not of the independent and the dependent. 'While
no one liberates himself by his own efforts alone, neither is he liberated
by others.'[77] The individual is not lost in the collective, but grows

through it.

It is only in these link-ups that individual social workers can participate in the analysis and redefinition of specific liberation groups. These social workers can identify their commitment to their colleagues in the work situation and begin to involve them by creating an awareness of the knowledge and experience-building which is going on and of alternative resources. The private, for this group of social workers, becomes professionally relevant.[78] The demand to come out in this sense is made of gay people in the Gay Issue of 'Case Con'.[79] But the strain of living in the open is considerable,[80] and can usually only be tolerated where there is support from an outside group.

The left-wing radical social worker who cannot relate to a base experience – and this affects all of us in some aspects of our work – is problematic. They may have a valuable understanding of the way in which current theories are structured and skills used, an academic facility in identifying issues or courses of action, but they are always prone to paternalism. An acceptance of the political nature of the social worker–client relationship is insufficient protection.

> It happens, however, that as they [the oppressors] cease to be exploiters or indifferent spectators or simply the heirs of exploitations and move to the side of the exploited, they almost always bring with them the marks of their origin; their prejudices and their deformations which include a lack of confidence in people's ability to think, to want and to know.[81]

They see themselves as leaders. In part this may be the reason for American social workers' disillusion with their alliance with the client groups and the liberation movements and the latter's disillusion with social work. The object of the alliance seems to have been to bring more power to social work, albeit that, had it been successful, the power acquired would have been used to forward the 'interests of the client'.[82] The left-wing radical seeks not power for a professional group to use on someone else's behalf, but accepts that in the long term the profession itself will undergo changes which would involve the loss of whatever power they had acquired to the people who use the services.

In the short term one of the tasks is to ensure that the work of radical movements outside social work is drawn into it, and traditional theory and guidelines for practice are reassessed. This will not change the functions allocated to social work, but may influence the way they are undertaken, and points where movement is possible can be identified and used. It is to this task that the following chapters attempt to make a contribution.

2

Values and social work

Economic and humanitarian values

Social work subscribes to a humanitarian value system, but whilst
values may in a limited sense have an independent existence their
detailed formulation in a specific society, or by a group within that
society, is influenced by the socio-economic structures as they exist
at a particular historical period. Once moved from the level of a
rallying cry, terms like 'freedom' and 'equality' reveal conceptions of
the good society and the good life which will vary because they have
different ideological foundations.

This is not an exclusively Marxist position. Talcott Parsons
thought that values have 'to legitimise a structural complex by which
economic production and the needs of households are simultaneously
met'.[1] Ultimate values have to be formulated in a way which meets this
end. They are underpinned at a lower level in terms of valued means and
behaviour. The second order rules of the society, for example statute
and legal precedent, make explicit which means and behaviour are
required, as opposed to being considered desirable.[2] Too frequently the
values to which social work subscribes are seen as autonomous[3] of both
ideology and the economic value system of Britain. Discussion is encapsulated, it is internal to the profession and to one system. If problems
arise, their origin is seen as located outside social work, or because
appropriate attitudes are absent in outsiders. Whilst respect for persons
and self-determination are often balanced with the good of the community the impact on these values of economic individualism, of achievement
through competition with others, is ignored. Similarly, control functions

21

are sometimes seen to create a problem for social work, whereas if fitted into, not separated from, the wider view, they become the implications of a society's specific formulation of values at the level of second order rules. These rules, which it is one of the functions of social work, among other groups, to implement, are not the result of consulting a single system of values – the humanitarian – they are the product of an inter-play between it and the economic values. They have an ideological, not neutral base. The social worker has to face the effects of the complex interaction between these two systems in a capitalist society on the lives of their clients, on the way social policy is formulated and how their own work is perceived. It is as important to recognise that humanitarian values do not predominate in these exchanges as it is to identify interaction.

Social values in context

If values have a legitimising function, it is logical that, as a society changes, values will need redefining from time to time. Changes need not be slight movements in interpretations, they can be major shifts. Tawney[4] traced one such change in the sixteenth and seventeenth century from social obligation to individual responsibility as the dominant value. This in turn required the validation of acquisitiveness and economic individualism as desirable human characteristics. He writes, 'plunged into the cleansing waters of later Puritanism, the qualities which less enlightened ages had denounced as social vices emerged as economic virtues. They emerged as moral virtues as well.'[5]

In the contemporary situation it is this specific formulation of freedom that the liberation movements and philosophers like Marcuse condemn.[6] The liberation movements which began by appealing to humanitarian values to demonstrate the injustice of their own position,[7] gradually found in them a source of their own oppression. The freedom of one person, one nation, is the oppression and poverty of another. Marcuse writes that he is hesitant to use the word 'because it is precisely in the name of "freedom" that crimes against humanity are being perpetuated'. In the first world, freedom to consume and sexual freedom can be enjoyed at the cost of becoming party to 'voluntary servitude'[8] and the 'administered life'.[9] For Marcuse, 'the truth is that this freedom and satisfaction are transforming the earth into a hell.'[10] To the liberal a recognition of the freedom-hell is an indicator of the need for a reassessment of old values or a search for new ones which will take into account a changed and changing society. The current general interest in values indicates that some such movements are occurring, but the left-wing radical sees any new formulation as unavoidably reflecting and perpetuating the ideology of capitalism unless there is a change in the economic base. The issue is not whether reference is being made to the humanitarian or economic value system, because they are inextricably linked. Inevitably, this affects the way that welfare is seen by the radical. For instance, one of the problems examined by Marcuse is whether it is possible to avoid the productive union of a 'Welfare Through a Warfare State'.[11] Similarly, for David Cooper 'Bourgeois Welfare is farewell, a farewell said (or left unsaid) by the welfare worker to his or her client.'[12] In the conservative political arena the debate about welfare has produced phrases like the 'unacceptable face of capitalism' which revolve around a simultaneous concern that welfare values are undermining economic individualism. Social work has to operate with definitions which are dependent upon the preferred economic structure and to cope with the effects of a need to ensure that the rules under which it operates do not create too uncomfortable a balance between the economic and humanitarian value system as they are formulated. Irrespective of debates about the meaning of social need, it is not only impossible to develop a welfare system which meets common human needs, it is undesirable. Social workers may well affirm that an adequate income and housing is required for the profession to operate an effective preventative service,[13] but it is not the profession which defines the conditions under which it will practice, but the socio-economic structure and its ideology.

In a search for a solution to what is essentially a political problem some have turned to social philosophy for guidance, its aim being to clarify 'the nature of life in its moral aspects'[14] through reasoned, logical argument which tries to be objective and a-political. Problems for clarification, however, emerge from a specific historical situation. Their discussion on an abstract, theoretical plane removes neither the philosopher nor the problem from time and place. The very aim of elevating problems to a purely theoretical level is in itself problematic for a Marxist because

> the resolution of theoretical contradictions is possible only through practical means, only through the practical energies of man. Their resolution is by no means, therefore, the task only of the understanding, but is a real task of life, a task which philosophy was unable to accomplish precisely because it saw there a purely theoretical problem.[15]

Philosophy creates at least two difficulties for the left-wing radical. First, it begins and ends at an abstract level and the nearer it comes to

23

the situations in which social workers are involved the more irrelevant it becomes.[16] Second, specific formulations of concepts like liberty, freedom, equality and justice serve a function within capitalism as supportive social myths which are part of an ideology legitimating and perpetuating the status quo and the interests of the dominant class. This situation is maintained not simply because of their control over the sources of production but because of an accompanying control over ideas and knowledge. Hence Marx claims that 'the ideas of the ruling class are, in every age, the ruling ideas: i.e. the class which is the dominant *material* force in society is at the same time the dominant *intellectual* force.'[17]

No problems are created for the social worker who sees capitalism as predominantly in the best interests of all people. For instance, Biesteck neatly brings the two together in a discussion about instrumental values by using the following metaphor: 'In terms of a profit-making enterprise, the benefits of partnership in human society are unbelievably lucrative, much more lucrative than a monetary investment reaping compound interest.'[18] There is an essential harmony even though there are points of stress or dis-ease. This view tends to lead to problems experienced being located mainly in the individual as opposed to being seen as the result of the socio-economic structure.[19] For a social worker committed to a socialist ideology the picture is quite different. Because values, as formulated and implemented, are seen as essential supports to the socio-economic order, major as opposed to minor problems are created for individuals and groups not belonging to the privileged minority. Moreover, some at least of the problems in relationships between persons are seen to arise from the impact of the economic values on relationships. The legitimated goal to own property extends beyond things, it embraces people.[20] 'My wife', 'my husband', 'my children' can be regarded and treated like things possessed. Indeed, clear 'possession' is seen by Anna Freud to be an important positive factor in adoption and the necessity to share a child with biological parents and agency a negative in foster care.[21] The literature on women clearly makes the link between marital fidelity and beauty with the exclusive possession of a desirable object. The world of relationships is not, therefore, seen as an uncontaminated area but as deeply penetrated by economic values.

It is hardly surprising that some radicals use appeals to values as a tactic. Alinsky, whose political creed was somewhat idiosyncratic, listed as one of his rules for radical action, the clothing of causes in the cloak of morality. Instead of appearing to be major challenges to the status quo, the objective is to make aims and demands appear consistent with the humanitarian values which are espoused at least at the unspecified level of the banner cry. Support is then more likely to come from liberals whose consciences are pricked by the exposure of social and human situations which are in direct contradiction with values such as equality, justice, freedom. It is to be noted, however, that Alinsky did not think that appealing to values had any direct bargaining power.[22] There is an important distinction between the conservative's and liberal's belief in social values as goals towards which a capitalist society can and should work, and an analysis which sees at best only partial concessions being possible. In a system based on private property, production for profit and the market mechanism, welfare is both minimal and concessionary, because individualism, acquisitiveness and competition are in direct opposition to the values that make it possible to put welfare in a central position — co-operation and solidarity.[23]

Respect for persons and economic individualism

The impact of the economic value system on social work can be illustrated by respect for persons. Whilst on a human level it is an expression of social or collective concern and caring, with individualisation being social work's practical expression, in British society it operates alongside economic individualism. The emphasis here is not on using a person's ability for the benefit of all, but on individual achievement, competition between individuals and groups for a piece of the cake, and status accorded to independence based on the possession or ownership of private wealth and power. Social workers affirm their belief in the worth of each person by virtue of their humanity and see them as having needs in common, but the society in which they operate distributes rewards unequally, not because of faulty mechanisms which can be remedied by social work or reform, but because the allocation of rewards is intended to operate in this way.[24]

The liberal, Kantian view of freedom to which social work subscribes[25] legitimates this situation by separating the public from the private person. The key issue to emerge is the extent to which individual, private freedom can be preserved in the face of a person's social existence.[26] It is to the questions arising from this formulation that social work has tended to direct itself in the past. True, the idea of interdependence is commonly emphasised, but discussion is often confined in two ways. First, it is limited to the micro-social situation — the family, the small group, the institution — the links between the micro-situation and the macro-situation are not made. Second, the most analysed dimension within the micro-situation is the significance of emotional and psychological interdependence. Evidence of poverty, poor housing, inadequate income can thus be seen as signs of social injustice or malfunctioning in a basically caring society that need to be remedied, instead of the inevitable consequences of economic individualism. If this value is accepted the issue for examination becomes what degree of social distress has to be tolerated in order to preserve economic individualism and its relation, freedom of choice. Within this scheme of things poverty has a positive function: 'If the poor are not poor through their own inadequacies, then I cannot rise by my own efforts.'[27]

There is a general resistance to exploring the interdependence of social groups upon each other — the economic dependence of the employer upon his workers for his own wealth and status — or the similarities between tax evasion and abuse of supplementary benefits, for instance. Such exercises are seen as irrelevant, misleading or simply confusing. A vertical view, as opposed to a horizontal view, of the inter-relationships between classes and groups is encouraged. Additional power is given to the vertical view of interdependence by the way questions are phrased. The issue becomes why some people fail, rather than how others manage to cope in spite of all the external pressures upon them,[28] the victim is still to blame.[29] There is a vast amount of research on the lives of those with social problems, but it is scarce in relation to the lives of those in the higher socio-economic groups. For the latter the major source is the press and biography, the material is anecdotal, not structured in terms of personal pathology or morality. Psychoanalytic literature, whose case material for the main part must be drawn from these groups, deals with the unconscious, not with social problems or the costs they create for others in the same society.

This context crucially affects social work in a number of areas, only three of which will be referred to here. As part of the welfare system social work is involved in the debate about residual, as opposed to universal, welfare. This is often framed in terms of expense, although money is only one factor; there is also the cost to economic individualism. The argument for residual welfare is based on the assumption that it is desirable and possible for everyone to acquire an adequate income to cope with their own social and economic needs and those of their immediate dependants, except in carefully defined situations. This position is not undermined by a recognition that certain groups are disadvantaged, and currently efforts are being made to reduce the impediments resulting from a person's race, sex or membership of a one-parent family. In contrast, universalists begin with a different interpretation of individual freedom. They see the free development of the individual as being linked to the active co-operation of others, because man is a social animal who cannot be neatly divided into private and public person. As a social animal, personhood is affirmed, not lost, through social and collective action; it is achieved not through competition with others — a mirror of the market place — but through mutual dependence on the needs of others.[30]

In contrast with social action orientations, relationship work has been seen as a 'neutral area' of activity, because relationships were located in the private or personal sphere of life. This contention must be the subject of debate because it has been seriously undermined by work which clearly identifies the effects of economic values on relationships, and proves that it is within the private as well as the public sphere that oppression is experienced. The analysis affects both class groups and blacks, women, children and gays. Hence the assertion that the personal is political. A corollary is that what is considered desirable or normal behaviour is also a political statement because behaviour and its interpretation has to be related to context.[31]

Finally, collective experience outside certain situations, such as school, work, play groups, tends to be equated with the production of personal uniformity as an intended or unintended consequence. Thus, residential, and, to a large extent, day-care situations are in the main seen as inherently inferior and unfortunate necessities when the family fails. The confusion is increased by the lack of distinction made between the concepts of the mass and the collective. We in Britain live and work in a mass consumer society and it is against this loss of identity and significance that local action and pressure groups of a wide variety of political opinions struggle. The collective situation can in no way be equated with living in a mass.[32]

In practice, respect for persons is daily negated by the effects of economic individualism, and the consequent powerlessness of many clients to resolve, by their individual efforts, the problems created, for instance, by inadequate income, housing, or by unemployment. Both nationally and internationally, there is a combination of want in the midst of plenty. Quite apart from whether social work is the appropriate medium to tackle these problems, it is implicit that to demand what privileged groups require as basic necessities is to seek utopia if those who are without ask for the same. To one a decent home and income is not a privilege but an assumption, for others it is an unrealistic, outrageous demand. Only small concessions are possible. Social workers are placed in an almost impossible dilemma by subscribing at one and the same time to a concept of freedom that places individuals in opposition with each other when their activities focus on the inter-relationships of the individual and society, and vice versa. While freedom is seen as being maintained by minimal interference, the situations they encounter indicate the necessity of major intervention to provide even the basis from which to promote it.[33] In the liberal abstract sense it has meaning only for those who possess the economic resources and social status on which its implementation depends. Theoretical attempts to resolve the dilemma for social work frequently extract people from their historical situation and from political ideologies. The good society is described as one in which people can develop their potential. The ideal becomes the acceptable face of capitalism — capitalism without the effects of competition and all that it entails. It is to seek the impossible and the goal is capitalism with all its essential parts removed.

Self-determination

The debate in social work about self-determination similarly shows how closely the development of expressed instrumental values ties in with the wider society. Although in evidence earlier, the main move from the term 'client participation' came in the 1930s. Perlman recalls that what

> we as social workers saw for the first time was that people like ourselves in backgrounds, social status, education, mores . . . were suddenly subject to circumstances that despite our lip service to the contrary we had reserved for people who were not like us.[34]

There is an echo here of Talcott Parsons's view that conceptions of the good society are concerned with ideas based on 'our kind of people'.[35] It is to the credit of social work that the application of this idea was extended to work with the poor, but even on a theoretical level it has caused endless problems. Maturity and choice seem to be crucial to the exercise of self-determination, and Biesteck is one of the few writers who does not get involved in conflicts about the limitations which exist in practice because he sees society as at present ordered as essentially good and in the best interests of its citizens. For him a heavy responsibility rests upon the social worker who is the 'knower' to ensure that appropriate limitations are set on clients' choices. His model is a simple one in which knowledge and maturity are seen to exist in the social worker who acts as a guide in a world of limited choices and freedom.[36] Others who are acutely conscious of the need for extensive social and economic reforms find themselves in greater difficulty.

The concept of self-determination is vital for Perlman[37] because even though choice is more illusory than real it is the 'very essence of human maturity'. She laments both the rich adolescent who has too many choices and the poor who have too few. There are certain conditions set out for the operation of mature choice: the problem must be seen realistically — by whose definition one wonders? — and 'perception must be clear and to be realistic must be free from distortions created by excess need or stress'.[38] The poor who cannot meet these conditions become, to use her term, 'faceless'. Bernstein also sees the impulsion to self-determination as a need or a drive in people in our society and thinks that it can be used as a rough guide to normalcy. In addition to the poor he refers to the special limitations placed on other groups — the handicapped, the retarded, the prisoner, and minority groups. The function of the social worker is to give them 'a voice'.[39]

However regretful these authors find their logic, they seem to be saying that in our society those who have too few or only pseudo-choices must be, or become, immature. This classification refers not to individuals but to large groups of people with whom social workers come into contact. Each of these writers appears to move from a model of determining man who makes decisions about life situations — the experiencing man of the existentialists — into the world of the economics of choice. Choice appears to be used in the economic sense, and a healthy economy, like a mature individual, has neither too much nor too little choice. The rich and poor, like all extremes, must become immature and the golden mean of the bourgeoisie remains the ideal. A concern with social injustice leads to an illiberal conclusion which gives absolute justification to both the paternalistic organisation and administration of welfare services, which are directed in the main towards the poor. If the poor are by definition immature, they will need both help and control. They cannot take part in major decisions about their fate because, suffering from severe economic pressures, their decisions will be immature. Rather than being central, large groups become marginal as people. Having failed to achieve in the economic world, they fail as human beings too through the adoption of an idea of maturity which is heavily contaminated by ideas of the market place. In part this may be one of the reasons for Alan Keith Lucas's feeling that 'social work has never really tried to treat people as subjects; it has gotten outside of them too fast, looking at them and not with them'.[40] The approach, moreover starts from the opposite end of the scale from consciousness-raising which begins with an attempt to redefine a situation from the inside, from the experience of the people in poverty or oppression. While not under-estimating the size and nature of the task, it carries a commitment to the belief in the power of the powerless and in their ability to undertake the work and succeed.[41]

High-level theory and practice

If there are problems at the high level of theory it is not surprising that in practice they are multiplied so many times that there seems to be a complete gulf between what is identified theoretically by the profession and its import for the practitioner. True, values are about objectives, ultimate goals and ideals, but the question remains as to how these are to be interpreted and used at the level of practice. Talcott Parsons clearly identifies the issue which is wider than social work. Value patterns, he writes, exist at a

> very high level of generality, without any specifications of functions or any level of internal differentiation, or particularity of situation . . . The individual is left with a great deal of responsibility, for not only achieving within the institutionalised normative order, but for his own interpretations of its meaning and of his obligations in it and to it.[42]

It is at these lower levels that social workers operate, and not only one person or department is involved. The individual social worker's interpretation in a specific situation may or may not differ from that of a senior, from a policeman or a teacher, from a client or a neighbour who is also involved. For the purposes of analysis it is possible to control the number of variables, in practice it is not. One task is at least to recognise that these variables exist, to identify them and their possible implications for any action planned, rather than standing back on the superiority of one's own or the professions's position.

Another task is to recognise that at this level social workers with similar class, professional and ideological backgrounds will not necessarily find themselves in agreement about value priorities in specific and complex situations which arise in their day-to-day work. The experience of discovering profound difference when accord was assumed can be stressful to the worker.[43] The problem arises where social workers are encouraged to see values as isolated absolutes operating in a static framework within a single frame of reference. Practice, like the rest of life, faces dynamic situations where a number of values apply, have to be ordered and may conflict with each other.

Many who saw in social work's allegiance to humanitarian values the strength and opportunity to develop a more caring society, become disillusioned when they discover the nature of the task has been incorrectly defined.[44] There is no wide open frontier, but a battle ground.[45] Though concessions may be wrested by working-class struggles, they are specifically formulated in a way consistent with continuing capitalism. The failure of social work to place its discussions in the context of the wider society cannot be resolved simply by pairing values – the individual's good with that of the community[46] – because this still excludes the interaction of the economic value system with humanitarian values. In addition, even within this limited framework, discussions often seem to imply that it is within the power of social work to find the correct measure of checks and balances to achieve an equilibrium, and to implement them. The world of work leads to rapid disillusionment, because the ground to be covered has not been clearly identified.

The client and values

The problem of lifting social work values out of the socio-economic context does not originate solely from what has become known as the psychoanalytic deluge. It has been demonstrated that social reform and policy remained a concern of social workers throughout that period.[47] Within social work, proposed reforms until recently were rarely accompanied by an analysis of the possible reactions to them of the economic and ideological structure, still less of the complex reasons for reforms becoming acceptable or even necessary. In accepting what seemed to be an uncomplicated, isolated position of embodying humanitarian concern, social work has allowed itself to become the active arm, as philosophy is the passive arm, for resolving social problems. To a large extent those issues on which a social work response is sought are based not on a commitment to meeting common human needs, but on the social problems created by and for those who are oppressed because of their class, or the position they occupy and the negative valuation placed upon them. The situation is more complex than a distaste for or a rejection of the practice of labelling particular groups of people. Clients' lives are crucially affected by a system of statutory and non-statutory regulations, sometimes called administrative law, which does not apply to those remaining outside the welfare system. The impact of administrative law on the day-to-day existence of certain groups, and specifically the poor, is greater than statute law.[48] An American study illustrates its effects on the lives of clients.[49] Although no British study is known to the writer, there are parallels. Social workers' clients who receive supplementary benefits are subject to a range of regulations which, until recently,[50] it was difficult to discover. The examples cannot be confined to social security; social work clients do not always know of the existence of regulations which are likely to affect the way their case is handled, and various departments interpret and use the same regulations differently. Sometimes inordinate difficulty is encountered in obtaining quite basic information such as whether a child is in care voluntarily or under Section II.

Although discretionary powers in social work and other departments have the merit of making creative justice a possibility,[51] there is the disadvantage of unpredictability for the client who is the potential receiver. Discretion is, moreover, not exercised over items of luxury provision, but on basic requirements against a background of accepted inadequacy of provision. What is often called the exercise of discretion is in fact a device for rationing scarce resources. Those who fail, either by individual or family effort, to provide for themselves become clients and are the subjects of a distinct system. Ideas of equality and parity are irrelevant because it is specific to a group and its existence and validity confirms both their difference and their dependence. Ironically, the stress on individualisation carries with it the tendency to separate where common cause is often more appropriate. It sometimes creates increased dependency on social work and its existing solutions because the development of alternative community supports are not encouraged.

Words and values

Within welfare there is a recognition of the existence of need and at the same time a negative valuation placed upon the needy. This is accompanied by a value being placed on self-help. Limitations of language are not entirely responsible for the current use of the term 'self-help' to describe groups which are essentially working co-operatively. Their activities are absorbed into the existing, approved framework and much of the import of their work is ignored. It is worth noting in passing that the substitution of the word 'consumer' for 'client' as a more neutral description of those coming to social workers is in fact the opposite, because it places welfare, whether experienced in terms of relationships or services, firmly in the framework of production-consumption, and thence into the hands of the cost-benefit analysts.[52] Welfare is justified not on the grounds of need, but because it pays for itself.

Emmanuel Tropp finds little to justify the retention of the word 'client', which in its Latin roots means follower or one leaning upon another for protection. The dependency element remains in two of the three definitions given in Webster and Roget's dictionary, and the third included the element of the customer or buyer seeking professional advice. Here the retention of independence is possible because money, a sign of social competence, is used. Tropp thinks that the word has been too contaminated by connotations of dependence to mean anything other than a person who is not self-reliant and by implication in our society someone not worthy of much respect. Those participating in collective activities are usually referred to as 'members' and he favours this as a substitute term in order for all involved to develop new perceptions of themselves and their work.[53] But definitions cannot of themselves create change nor can they be imposed. At present it is sufficient to note that 'advocate' seems to have emerged in recognition of the hazards involved in using or receiving welfare services[54] which place clients under a specific and complex system of administrative law or regulations. The advocate, or an outside person, who gives a second opinion to the client, and not to the agency, is a necessary development where there is such a concentration of resources and power.

Social workers' values

In spite, or rather because, of its liberal tradition, British social work has a strong allegiance to the status quo, and the rapid increase in the statutory powers and duties currently being allocated to it will intensify the relationship, and in consequence separate further the social worker from clients. Some writers are quite clear that at present social work is primarily concerned with social control and that the question is: what are the future possibilities?[55] Any search for alternatives inevitably involves a shift from a preoccupation with developing appropriate attitudes for particular situations or identifying instrumental values back to a more detailed examination of the values on which social work is based. If the direction sought is to see social work as a change agent, simple reassertions of values as absolutes requiring little explanation are no longer sufficient. Analysis outside social work has politicised change orientations, whether the object is relationships or policies. The concern of social work for people in distress, its analysis of those situations and the range of alternatives open are no longer seen as emanating simply from humanitarian values which are neutral. They have been connected with economic structure and ideology, with class, race and sex.

Moreover, a change orientation brings personal values to the fore and begins to make explicit political commitments. Abstract appeals to terms like 'equality' raise few problems, but when the debate continues, arguments have to be more specific about meanings, and questions begin to be asked about means and institutions, the extent of the change and its perceived implications. To focus on change, as opposed to adjustment or manoeuvring within an existing structure, is a political act because it involves decisions about directions for social development and priorities and the way to achieve them. The problem for social work is that it will divide and separate because these decisions, which ostensibly are about social, economic and relationship supports for clients, cannot be isolated from the repercussions obtaining these would have on the wider society. Whether these intended consequences are welcomed or not will depend on ideological positions. Irrespective of movements towards professionally acceptable attitudes and the possibility of increasing open-mindedness during training,[56] a person's central value system is not susceptible to rapid change. While a social worker may be able to develop accepting attitudes to an unemployed person, most will subscribe to the work ethic. Attempts to improve and humanise existing welfare provision frequently ignores a basic commitment to the values underpinning its continued inadequacy, even though social workers do not like the *effects* on the lives of their clients. Though condemning the low levels of supplementary benefits, the majority would reject a demand for a home and living wage based not on a person's productive capacity, their qualifications or academic status, but on their common human needs, nor would they accept the personal sacrifices this would entail in terms of lower income and standard of living. Economic individualism, self-sufficiency through work for wages, holds strong in social legislation and administrative law even when it can be clearly demonstrated that the fault cannot be remedied by individual effort. To this and the work ethic in the main the unemployed person, the family and the social worker hold.

The distaste for examining the personal value system of social workers is amply demonstrated by the paucity of work of this subject. The assertion seems to be that the commitment to humanitarian values can be maintained during working hours, and the personal values of the worker are not involved. It is necessary to examine what work exists in order to establish whether or not there seems to be continuity or difference between members' values and those of lay people. Only one study known to the writer relates to British social workers; it is focused not on values but on attitudes to black people and showed that social workers had a similar spread of attitudes to the general population.[57] A research project in America noted a change in the values of social workers after graduation towards those of the general public.[58] Another acknowledged that social science and humanities students tended to be more involved than others in social issues, and had within American society made a positive contribution to identifying moral issues. However, he goes on to state that the

corroding influences of materialistic society in which social work is practised appear to change the behaviour and the values of social workers and make their responses more nearly that of the general public despite professional goals which would suggest a different pattern.[59]

There is no reason to think that British social workers would present a greatly altered picture. The sceptic might comment that what could be happening is that apparent changes in values and attitudes during training were of a temporary and superficial nature, insufficient to withstand the pressures of the world of work or the conflicts created for the individual between their personal and the professional value system. Student radicalism is frequently a phenomenon pertaining to that period, and is often not based on a sound analysis of the position and function of social work in British society, the limitation placed on any radical action within it, or the wider consequences of attempting to implement changes. The failure to place the humanitarian values and aims of social work in the context in which they must operate is perhaps one of the reasons for the lament of a sociologist teaching social work students. He records that he found no difficulty with research findings that documented the failings of other professions or groups, but that 'inordinate difficulty arises when material is presented on social work, material relevant to themselves or more accurately their future selves'.[60]

Conclusion

The radical begins with a rejection of the liberal Kantian view of freedom, and sees both him or herself and fellow human beings achieving freedom and personhood in the context of the collective. In social work the aim is to work towards instrumental values which do not distinguish between social worker and client in a paternalistic way, but which affirm their common humanity. This is not to ignore either the dynamics of relationships or the insights into them brought by psychoanalysis and psychology, but a refusal to accept theoretical formulations which are divorced from experience and action. There is also an assertion of the interdependence of the micro- and the macro-social situation and a denial of their polarisation. Thus social work and its values are not isolated from their social context but a part of it.

It is above all necessary to avoid postulating 'society' once more as an abstraction confronting the individual . . . though man is a unique individual, a really individual social being — he is equally the whole, the subjective existence of society as thought and experienced.[61]

Social work cannot bridge the gap between individual and society,[62] because social work and the individual cannot stand aside. The magazine 'Case Con' places social work firmly in the world of work when it calls social service departments 'Seebohm factories'. It is possible that what is intended to be seen as a negative experience of work in large organisations and the accompanying feelings of powerlessness, may have a positive outcome. It could provide a base from which the increasing unionisation of social work can move towards forging links with other workers — their clients — and valuing solidarity above isolation and status.

Finally, the place of ideology cannot be ignored either in the formulation or implementation of values. Both have played a large part in maintaining the status quo. Appeals by social work to values are not therefore simple solutions to the problems faced 'since there is no independent ideology . . . the only choice is either bourgeois ideology or socialist ideology. There is no middle course.'[63] The ideology of social work is bourgeois and in a pre-revolutionary society it can be no other. Although individuals within the profession may reject it they can remain within social work or, for that matter, in any other social institution through conscience compromise.

3

THE family

Introduction

The family has a central position in social work theory and practice.
Literature abounds, but there is frequently a lack of two perspectives:
the historical and the cross-cultural. Without these, theories at the
lower level concerned with practice cannot identify what is to do with
methodology and what is ideology, or indeed whether the two can be
separated. Practice can easily become an attempt to maintain the
dynamic institution of the family within a static framework. Agreement
with Bronfenbrenner that 'the family is, after all, the product of a
million years of evolution and should have some survival value for the
species'[1] should not preclude a recognition that the evolutionary
process does not come to a halt in the 1970s either for the family or
for society.

The family in microcosm

To examine only the way the functions of reproduction, socialisation,
economic and social support are currently allocated[2] is insufficient,
because a specific pattern can be explained only in terms of the larger
society.[3] This interaction is the reason why a wide variety of viable
patterns of family exist in the world today.[4] The concept of the
universality of the family is valid only in so far as account is taken of
these diverse patterns,[5] and when it is not used to force this diversity in
to a uniform shape, or prove the intrinsic superiority of a particular form.

37

Changes can occur in the way functions are allocated without the family being destroyed as a social institution, though a specific patterning of it may be dramatically altered over time. For instance, in industrial societies the functions currently thought to belong to nuclear families can be carried on in whole or part outside them. Some have been transferred temporarily during periods of crisis such as day care in war-time Britain, or permanently as in education where the main responsibility has become that of the school. Argument about actual or potential change in the nuclear family is often discussed within a framework which poses the issue of whether or not it is being destroyed or undermined in global terms and a specific patterning becomes confused with the family as a universal institution.

The current vehemence of attacks on, or defence of, the nuclear family is because it represents society in miniature,[6] even though its declared absolute evil or virtue appears to have little to do with the average family encountered by the social worker. The arguments are about the economic and patriarchal structure of society as they are reflected through and perpetuated by the family in microcosm. For the conservative this is the reason it must be preserved, at least for the time being, while for the left-wing radical it is the reason it must be changed.

The dynamic for change in the ideology and shape of the family does not come simply from left-wing or liberation movements — the pressures for change are complex and emanate in part from the existing capitalist system. Altered demands for labour supply could easily result in the validation of day care for young children and the consequent provision of creches by employers and the state.[7] There is already evidence of disillusion with the nuclear family as the main institution for socialisation. Increasingly, it is failing to provide the stability thought essential for this process to be satisfactorily accomplished and the rapidity of social change is seen to create problems between parent and adolescent because acquired parental knowledge relates to a past situation and not that encountered by the young.[8] It has been argued by Juliet Mitchell that, with the extension of the school-age range to both the below 5-year-olds and above 15-year-olds, the school and not the family could become the main ideological institution. She considers the nuclear family is already redundant within capitalism and its very weakness is the reason it is both supported and attacked.[9]

While it would be inaccurate to claim that these issues are not raised in social work education, they are often confined to disciplines impinging on social work, and not integrated into its own theory. Here there is a tendency to start with an assumption of the correctness of our current family pattern and to rapidly move in focus onto either intra-family relationships or the differences between individual family units. Family functioning at these levels is assessed and their health-producing or pathogenic potential analysed and compared. Paradoxically, concentration on these dimensions, as opposed to its dynamic inter-relationship as a social institution with society,[10] leads to the family which receives so much attention from social workers having its societal significance under-estimated.

The macrocosm of the family

Through the social institution of the family, in Britain the nuclear family, new members receive a place in society and are legitimated as members of it. Appeals to progressive attitudes towards children born outside marriage are of little avail when the social rules are examined. A child born without a *social* father in Britain has no legal relatives and it is a matter of dispute whether or not it has legal siblings. A child born abroad to a single British mother has no right to a place in British society, no right to the nationality of the mother — the dyad of the mother-child does not enable the child to make an unequivocable entry, the presence of a social father does.[11] Legitimacy through his presence gives a recognised claim to inherit the wealth and property of kin as well as a place among them. The laws of inheritance are inextricably bound up with the laws of legitimacy and the requirement for monogamy seeks to ensure that the man is certain that the child who receives these benefits is his own. The sexual fidelity of the woman, the double standard of morality, have to be related to this transfer of the status of legitimacy and, in general, property through the male and marriage relationships. Within this frame of reference it was logical that until recently adultery on the part of the husband was not considered adequate grounds for divorce, whereas for the wife it was.[12] A second function specific to the family is that it is a base from which new alliances and new units are established through marriage. The incest taboo ensures that marriage takes place not only outside the biological unit, but outside important kin relationships. The significance of kin remains firm at marriage in the prohibited degrees and usually in their physical presence. In most human societies men exchange women, and the father or brother of the bride still 'gives her away'.[13] Several writers have commented on the decrease in the significance of kin in modern Britain and the United States. While some have focused on the support the nuclear family received from them in the past, and to a large extent still does, others have turned their attention towards the decline in the control exercised by kin over the sexual, marital and parenting behaviour of nuclear family members. The area requires study,[14] because, having identified a problem, solutions are being sought which either seek a substitute through increased state control and hence intervention in family life,[15] or the building of alternative systems of kin whose basis extends beyond the traditionally defined boundaries.[16]

The family also acts as one of the sources of stability in social stratification. Frank Parkin[17] has illustrated how class influences the expectations parents have of their children, and how in societies which attempt 'to cream off talent' the family plays a somewhat subversive part. Working-class parents tend not to encourage high aspirations in their children either at school or work. For the majority this is a realistic assessment of the limited opportunities open to them, because movement mainly takes place at the margins of the social classes. In consequence, the family, together with other social institutions and the local community, provides a useful and humane system for preparing the working-class youth for their future. Those without privilege are not inclined to reject their status because the reasons for it are not clear and its sources are too complex: there is no 'transparency' of the connections between the causes and the consequences of the 'class situation',[18] nor of the family's part in it. The lack of transparency is made possible largely by ideology. The family is 'a place equally and freely to enjoy individual freedom and private property'.[19] The fact that the socio-economic structure militates against this for large groups of people who cannot find a place to live in, quite apart from buying one, does not undermine the ideology; the hope remains.

The biological nuclear family

The failure to place the biological nuclear family in a wider historical context creates a vision of an entity that arose phoenix-like from the fact of human reproductive biology.[20] Eric Raynor's father stands at the primeval 'cave door',[21] the implication being that the modern family is but a stone's throw away from prehistory.[22] But the biological requirement for two adults of the opposite sex for conception and biological parenthood to occur cannot be taken as the sole origin of the family as a social institution. Talcott Parsons writes of this tendency of the social sciences to see in 'the universality and the constancy of the structure of the nuclear family, a simple reflection of its biological function and composition', whereas the two biological bases, sex and generation, are 'points of reference'.[23] Kinship patterns, and not the biological unit, are for Lévi-Strauss the features that distinguish human society; the 'biological base must be transformed if society is to be instituted'.[24] In other words the circular pattern of relationships within the biological unit has to be broken and connections established with other families. The process by which this is achieved is through the institution of marriage. New relationships are made between the man, the woman and their respective families. Lévi-Strauss sees these steps as necessary for culture to be established.[25] The modern form of the biological nuclear family is a phenomenon of industrial capitalism, not the result of a return to nature or of biological imperatives, even though we have become accustomed to loving and hating it. The social affirmation of the biological aspects are severely circumscribed by culture, for instance only parenthood and, until recently, sex within marriage are socially legitimated. The single mother or the child of an adulterous union are not regarded as expressions of human biology that can receive unreserved social approval or legitimation. It is not the intrinsic qualities of biological parenthood that are valued, but only those socially instituted or superimposed upon it.[26]

Because of experience in situations where there is a weak or broken connection, and because of their involvement in developing and maintaining parenting situations which fall outside, the social work profession does not like to be accused of over-valuing the blood tie. But it is impossible to avoid the social significance derived from the way it links with the laws of legitimacy and inheritance, or the fact that all of these are wedded to the modern nuclear ideal. The current re-evaluation of the status of substitute care is less a symptom of the validation of foster or adoptive care as real alternatives to the biological unit than the result of a disquiet about the capacity of some nuclear families to accomplish successfully child-care tasks as they are defined in contemporary Britain, in particular, the poor and one-parent families. More than attempts to prevent non-accident injury to children are involved. A major impetus comes from a desire to reaffirm the importance of stability in the nuclear unit, even if it is at the expense of losing, in some cases, its biological component, as the pattern which is most likely to produce the desired type of adult. At the same time this unit is the least likely to require social and economic changes because it is the legitimated pattern for family life and as such is the reference point for welfare provision. Usually included in the criteria for the selection of adoptive and foster parents are marital and economic stability, although in practice they are inaccurate predictors.[27] Fewer issues are raised than if one-parent families, complex family structures and communes were given social approval as alternatives, or if attempts were made to improve the economic circumstances of people parenting in poverty.

The historical perspective

Without a knowledge of history it is impossible to evaluate these developments, and this perspective is often missing in social work. There is no lack of theoretical material. Social historians,[28] sociologists,[29] and lawyers[30] have provided documentation and a dictionary will show how the word 'family' has changed in meaning.[31] Social work has tended to accept the nuclear family as both the norm and the ideal in the absolute sense and has moved quickly on to concentrate on description and analysis within this framework. Social work does not stand alone, however. Cuber concludes that some of his fellow sociologists have accepted the traditional legal and religious structures as basic assumptions as though they were 'eternal values' and not specific to a model in a particular culture at a point in time. In presenting this static model they have become, he thinks, 'apologists for a structural system already somewhat passé'.[32]

The social institution of the family is responsive to changes in society, irrespective of whether these are seen as social or economic in their origin. Expectations of the family also change. Not only does the modern family include a member or members who are producers, it is now, at the same time, important as a consumer of products. While under early capitalism the function of the family was to provide large numbers of unskilled workers for the production of scarce resources, the contemporary good family is expected by both technologists and child development experts to raise children, not too many in number, who are educated, disciplined, independent and who have internalised controls.[33]

Models: *de jure* and *de facto*

The gap between the *de jure* and the *de facto* system of the family has also been identified by Cuber. In complex and changing societies this can be wide, and guidelines for practitioners, which are derived from the *de jure* system, often appear to have very little to do with what exists in their own or their clients' lives, even though they may both experience guilt about these departures. A list compiled by Cuber of the *de jure* system is part of every social worker's stock in trade: the oughts are monogamous, lifelong marriage with those ending before deemed to have failed, the nuclear family is the unit for nurture, economic support, consumption, the acquisition and inheritance of property; legitimacy is, in addition, possible only within marriage and there are certain expectations about the allocation of functions according to sex which are validated socially in the concept of roles; in spite of birth control, the sexual monopoly of the wife remains in order to ensure that children are biologically the husband's.[34]

The ideal model of the nuclear family is united and stable, boundaries are set to the social and economic responsibilities for its members as well as around its interactive relationship patterns, but as soon as it is linked to the larger society it becomes disunited. Members work for different bosses in different places, they go to work, to school or stay at home. With shift-work they will wake, sleep and eat at different times, and the individual patterns of their lives are in conflict, as any family who has a member involved in shift-work or night-cleaning will know.

The family is also divided by the requirement laid upon it to achieve, at the same time, solidarity and the maximum development of each of its members. Laing's work clearly illustrates how individuals in the same family can be in conflict with each other in an attempt to achieve cohesiveness, self-realisation, and separateness.[36] These conflicts between individuals in the family, specifically those between parents and children, are becoming institutionalised. Children's interests are no longer seen by all as coincidental with the biological nuclear family unit, and the conflict has been generalised from issues connected with child abuse and neglect. Separate rights are sought for all children, which are not simply the rights of protection from physical and emotional harm accorded in our society to those who are in certain weak or dependent positions.

The extent of the discordance between children and their biological parents is indicated by the demand that the latter need education for a specialised job, and skills which cannot be acquired through the now discredited maternal instinct or through the process of social living. Two different concepts of freedom are being applied to two parties in the same unit. Liberals have traditionally opted for the negative concept,[37] but now while their parents continue to have only negative rights — the freedom from hindrance in pursuit of the optimum conditions for their children — children are being accorded positive rights to conditions which are growth-promoting in every sense. Placed within the societal context the end-result is not an unequivocal move towards better child care but one further step in a process of justifying and legitimating the transfer of children from poor economic and social backgrounds to substitute homes which come closer to the desired nuclear model by incorporating both stability and economic security.[38]

There are indications that eventually this may involve not only guidelines for assessing who is and who is not a 'good parent', or educating people who decide to become or are already parents, but ultimately decisions about who should be a parent. British and

American literature on the family is beginning to share a presumption that either people's interest in becoming parents must decline or it will be necessary to regulate their desire in some other way. The Director of the National Children's Bureau raised the question obliquely at their annual conference in 1975. She wondered why 'we assume that the light of nature is sufficient for parents to know what the needs of children are and how these are best met'.[39] Another speaker commented on the fact that although a demonstration of minimum fitness is required to drive a car, none is needed to become a parent. He went on to accept that 'This implies a challenge . . . to the absolute right of parents to bring children into the world, educate them as they wish and yet remain totally untrained for their role.'[40] Both speakers leave untouched what happens to those who fail to achieve the minimum standard, who decides the curriculum and undertakes the assessment. It is at this point that Margaret Mead[41] and Leo Davids[42] take up the discussion. Both envisage a separation between couple or group marriage and parental marriage; only to the latter are conditions attached which have to be met by the couple. Emotional and social stability must be demonstrated to professionals who will also require satisfaction that the couple is able to give economic support to a child. Parenting, like work, becomes a specialised job. It is hard and can only be undertaken by the chosen and trained few.

It is vital to make a distinction between this position and that of those whose aim is to improve the quality of care given in individual families and adult-child relationships. There is more than one facet to child care. Erikson's work[43] illustrates the connection between child-care patterns and the type of adult person sought by a particular society. On this level the question becomes not 'is this good child care'? but 'is this the sort of society we want?' Equally significant for the profession is whether it wants to carry the sort of functions a strict regulating of parenting would require. Selection involves for Mead the use of interviews and predictive tests which someone would have to administer. Her assumption that these tests and skills exist is as alarming as her belief that they would be neutral. The full circle of the microcosm and the macrocosm of the family becomes complete.

Child development, class and ideology

The class implications of moves to control parenting, whether they remain only indicators of trends or become actualities, are obvious and have been pointed out by BASW and Holman.[44] The requirement for economic security is less likely to be met as social class declines. Child development studies also show that the working-class child does less well than the middle-class child on measurements of social adjustment and in attainment at school. There are also profound implications for those who deviate — the single mother, the parent on his or her own, the lesbian mother,[45] the political extremist, are but a few.

It is important to identify the class and ideological content of studies of children's development. This, far from invalidating them, rather alters the use to which they are put. Many provide interesting descriptions of the effects on children of the way material rewards and social approval are allocated in our society in favour of certain classes or groups, and denied others. This conclusion is consistent with the finding that social class is a highly significant factor in children's development,[46] in parenting behaviour[47] and in education.[48] It is at these points that the studies link with a structural analysis of society. Thus, the current emphasis on a child-centred approach is not without problems either for the theorist or the practitioner. Whilst there is no question that there is a need to minimise physical abuse towards children and to improve the quality of their lives, there is a danger that this valid area of concern will divert attention away from the parallel need to examine the structural pressures on the family at all class levels, and from the specific stresses experienced by the poor and other oppressed groups. Although expressed in different terminology, the fear is shared by many in social work.[49] Legislation[50] has reinforced this fear because 'without the development of adequate preventative services child "rescue" legislation which deals only with situations once children have been separated from their families is unbalanced and inappropriate.'[51]

Although the danger is clearly recognised by the professional association of social workers, it cannot be resolved by them, and the degree of their influence over the nature of its resolution is strictly limited. The context in which this situation arises is a society in which there is no parity of conditions for people in the different social classes, whether they are children or adults. There are the same expectations, but the opportunities to meet them decline with social class. Social work does not have the power to change this, but it can perform a useful function by documenting the disadvantages experienced by the lower socio-economic groups, by ethnic minorities or other families which do not conform to the stable nuclear family ideal. This information could be used to analyse the generic needs of people in parenting positions; that is those social and economic background supports all people who are caring for children require, irrespective of the family pattern in which they are living. Only subsequently is it possible to clarify specific needs required in addition to this base. At present the starting point is the second and not the first stage. One of the advantages of the liberation movements and collective support groups is their efforts to analyse and act upon the factors they find they have in common with each other. There is a growing knowledge about these generic factors in parenting upon which social work needs to draw, because, in contrast with children's needs, there is little information at present. Moreover, its investigation is problematic because it leads to questions, on the one hand, about the unequal distribution of resources required as a basis for parenting, and, on the other, about an analysis which limits the adequate performance of parenting and an adequate experience for the child within the confines of a nuclear unit.

Social work and the nuclear ideal

Although social work theory can be shown to depart at some points from the ideal, these are deviations in detail. The contemporary confusion is reflected, and social work is, therefore, limited in the number of solutions perceived to be viable ways of meeting children's and adults' needs. Implicit in most social work literature and practice is the belief that the biological, stable nuclear family is best. Why this position is taken and whether it is a relevant base from which to proceed in contemporary Britain cannot begin to be debated until the assumption has been made explicit. Then a major point for discussion will be whether the ideal is adopted simply because it is numerically dominant and socially valued at present or because it is considered to be the only model without emotional and social problems which are not intrinsically insurmountable.

If the biological, stable nuclear family is regarded as the ideal, the culmination of a process of historical evolution, all other models existing in contemporary Britain must be deemed to be failures to some degree. Efforts in practice and service provision will consequently be directed towards its maintenance and to minimising the inevitable damage incurred by those living outside this pattern. Quite different objectives emerge if a range of alternative models are considered viable, with each having problems but none insurmountable by virtue of the structure of the model. One factor militating against clarity in discussion is the use of the word 'nuclear' to describe a range of family situations for which it was not intended. Strictly speaking, the absence of a social father means that a single mother and her child are not covered by the term; whether a one-parent family headed by a formerly married man or woman qualifies is an unanswered question. The currency of the word 'incomplete' to describe both appears to give a negative answer; the commune, by intent, stands apart.

If social workers move towards recognising that all complex

societies contain a plurality of models, a number of tasks emerge. The first is to identify and document, alongside other groups, the specific social and economic disadvantages accruing to any one model. Standing by a proposition that there are a range of patterns for family life does not eliminate the fact that at present only one is socially and legally validated and that others by implication experience varying degrees of social and economic discrimination. The one-parent family, for instance, is likely to have a low income and be poorly housed; this, in addition to the social stigma, will affect those within it.

A second task is an examination of the problems created by the existence of a plurality of models. These are not, as is often implied, simply internal to the model itself, but arise because of their juxtaposition with others in the same society. The acceptance and tolerance of difference is not easy even in theoretical discussions about other societies' cultural patterns. The stress experienced by living and working in a multi-cultural society can be acute where there is an adherence to an ideal model; all falling outside its boundaries are necessarily excluded from the ultimate accolade of success. Social workers are potentially in a good position to contribute to this process of validating a range of family models and to encourage groups outside social work in this activity. A significant part of their work is in areas which fall outside the ideal model, or deals with its negative or dysfunctional aspects — the child, the adult, the old and young who are outside the nuclear family or are inadequately supported by it. Though intended to be a self-liquidating[52] group one of the negatives of the nuclear family is that the process can begin too early for the child or be accomplished too completely for the old.

Third, it is important to avoid the tendency in analysis to take the biological stable, nuclear family as the starting point because it distorts the way needs are defined and services planned. We live in a society where serial monogamy or serial polygyny[53] is occuring with increasing frequency, and to decry this fact will not make it vanish. It is insufficient to analyse situations using the nuclear family as the only frame of reference. The solutions evolved will simply concentrate on supporting the preferred model and coping with breakdowns in its functioning, instead of thinking of generic needs and the supplementary support families will need now if they remain outside the ideal or if moves are made between one model for family life and another. The myth of the normal family has long been questioned[54] and the challenge to the myth of the stable nuclear family as the only viable unit for children and adults has to be brought firmly into social thinking and its implications for theory and practice examined.

Finally, little of value will be accomplished if social workers are left with a number of isolated models as guidelines for their practice. While theoretical constructs respect the boundaries drawn around them, life does not. A child's or adult's life experience may encompass two or more models. The fact that change creates stress is an established dictum, but if there is an acceptance that such movements can be successfully accomplished, social workers could make a contribution towards those experiencing stress because they are moving between family models. A commitment to focus work on this area would involve research into what is involved in these changes and what ways through have been found.

A move towards explicitly accepting and supporting a range of models has to take into account the divergent opinions existing among members of the social work profession and of the wider context. The urgent desire to predict and to control the pattern of family life leads some to cast a retrospective glance towards an idealised type of extended family thought to exist in pre-industrial England, or to rural living. These ignore the fact that this pattern was a response to the historical context in which the family was located. It is not intended here to join the army of predictors of the family's future, but to state that the family is a dynamic institution with pressures upon it to change in response to new conditions. A number of viable patterns have emerged, others will probably develop, and evidence is beginning to challenge cherished assumptions.[55] Although within the life experience of increasing numbers of people, there is little sign of a move to legitimate a plurality of models, or any evidence that, if there is, such a move would be successful. On the contrary, there seems to be a reassertion of the stable nuclear model, albeit with some minor, in terms of the model, changes. The inclusion of substitute two-parent familities, whether foster or adoptive, is an acceptance of a degree of instability which it is intended to limit by confirmation of the substitute home. Until recently the preference for the nuclear model was implicit rather than explicit, and there were in consequence few declared hierarchies. The Curtis Report identified a clear order of precedence ranging from the child's own home, through substitute family to residential care.[56] In spite of warnings about institutionalising these hierarchies, they have had a profound effect on practice — that the family consists of the two biological parents who remain together was assumed rather than stated. The contemporary problem of the increasing number of marriages which are not life-long, and the increase in the number of single parents who keep their children, has brought a number of declarations in favour of trying to reconnect parenthood with the life long marriage. One influential person has categorically stated that 'single parenthood has little to recommend it where there is a choice'.[57] In 1972, Sir Keith Joseph, then Secretary of State, described the 'advantaged' home as one providing 'the child with consistent love and guidance, understanding and firmness—with a warm, loving, dependable relationship with two parents, in the early years, throughout childhood and through to independence'.[58]

The findings of the 1958 National Cohort studies[59] have been used by some as evidence to support the main model and at the same time absorb adoptive families into it. Adoption is seen 'as a contemporary institution . . . entirely validated by comparison of the groups of children born illegitimately who were adopted and who were not adopted.'[60] It is significant that the vindication is regarded as upheld in spite of the fact that social class and sex were found to be the most important factors influencing the development of children, and the adopted group was in the most economically advantaged position while those born outside marriage who were not adopted were living in the worst social and economic conditions. Once these are controlled, differences are 'greatly reduced' and in some cases disappear.[61] The failure to observe the basic rules of comparative analysis in the social sciences, where there is matching of groups for social and economic backgrounds in addition to age and birth status, is a symptom of the authors' commitment to an ideology of the family. Indeed, the single-parent family is excluded by one of them as a viable unit for child care, because even given optimal social and economic support the one-parent family 'can never wholly compensate for the social and psychological disadvantages. More than economics is involved.'[62] Some advocates of the stable nuclear model resort to the academic game of propounding only the positives of their own ideal, whilst describing the negatives of all other models. This creation of opposites fails to take into account that there are negatives inherent in any pattern of caring for all involved, and that negatives are for the non-nuclear models reinforced and aggravated by socio-economic factors. These act on families irrespective of whether there is one, two, three or four parenting adults involved. Parenting in poverty reduces many of the differences between the models, just as does the possession of wealth.

The popularity of marriage is sometimes taken as an indicator of the strength of the modern nuclear family but in Great Britain one in ten families (1971) are one-parent families[63] and in 1970 one in four children in America were living in this situation.[64] Like any other group, social workers are living with this reality in their personal lives, but are to some degree at least involved professionally in a denial of its viability. Statistically, marriage can be dubbed a success — the re-marriage rate is high. Given the current social climate, this is to be expected. Social pressures strongly favour conformity to the norm of married status and the repairing of a 'broken' marriage by forming a new one. It is generally assumed that children need two parents, whereas evidence now indicates that the children living with widowed mothers and fatherless illegitimate children do not differ significantly from other 11-year-olds in two-parent families of similar socio-economic backgrounds.[65] There is a psychological and social unpreparedness for being alone, and many women cannot earn enough to live on their own, quite apart from supporting children as well. Marriages need not, therefore, be contracted because a satisfying mutual relationship exists, but these pressures towards marriage need not retain their present intensity and there are indications that they are beginning to decrease.[66] Moreover, a detailed analysis of statistics shows that while for many the status of a divorced spouse is a temporary condition, for others it is likely to be more permanent. After divorce 64 per cent of men and 60 per cent of women remarry, but the percentage of widows and divorced women remarrying diminishes with the number of children they have: those with no children are the most likely to remarry.[67]

In a context of changing relationship patterns a re-assessment of the traditional emphasis on marital work becomes important. Artificial boundaries can be set up around knowledge about skills in relationship work which prevent the exploration of their relevance in a variety of situations where the label 'marital' is applied only with difficulty. The first assumption is that the relationship must have a heterosexual, not a homosexual, base, that it is a pair relationship and not a group of adults, either connected or not by past or present marriage relationships. The man or woman choosing to live alone is excluded in spite of the fact that he or she may have close emotional and sexual relationships with others. Similarly, those caring for children who decide not to remarry, frequently have to learn to maintain a relationship with the other parent who may or may not have a new partner. Others can be left with a series of unconnected islands of nuclear family or pair relationships when there is in reality a continuous narrative. Again, where children are involved, the ability to create and tolerate continuity is a key factor. The participants in therapy or casework, present or not, extend beyond the pair and in the case of the commune can be the total group. The task for some may be increasingly the development of inclusive, not exclusive, in-depth relationships currently thought to characterise a 'good' marriage.

Day-to-day concerns and the long term

Because social work operates in a capitalist structure which both creates and validates inequality, practice guidelines have been developed and are acted upon which take no account of inherent inequalities or their impact on family life. In the main, whether severe cases of child abuse are seen to arise from personal immaturity, class or specific group oppression will make little difference to an immediate decision to remove the child even where it is clear that there has been severe public neglect of parental needs. Few alternatives are available. When the social worker's decision is that the child's separation is the result of material or social resources, it is impossible for the interventive repertoire to include a prescription for an adequate home or income; similar limits are set on the range of alternative therapeutic help and on the available social support systems for a parent deemed to lack the internal emotional resources. At the moment all are the same because they do not have the chance to be different.

Guidelines for day-to-day practice have to be located in a context, and are not formed solely out of humanitarian concern; they represent a range of choices between the rights and responsibilities in the relation of each to the other and in respect of each to the wider society. Choices are themselves limited not only by what is thought to be therapeutically possible, or available, but by economic and social restraints placed on the development of alternative support systems. Where ideas of economic scarcity prevail, competition between parents for the available resources is inbuilt. Hence one writer concluded that if less money was spent on 'unwanted children' more would be available for the wanted.[68] Rather than recognising the need to develop mutual support systems for people in parenting positions, the tendency is to strive competitively to be better than each other. A key issue to be explored in social work is whether it is possible to move from being primarily concerned with protecting children in crises, towards participating in the creation of better parenting opportunities based on a knowledge of the generic needs of parenthood. There is evidence that in terms of effective intervention on the child's behalf it is less important to ensure a high level of expertise in people like social workers than to create 'opportunities for those who are potentially the most powerful in the child's life, his parents, his friends and immediate associates, to realise their potential'.[69]

4

The family: alternatives

Introduction

Radical social workers are faced by a lack of bridges between their day-to-day work with people and a political analysis of the family as a social institution with ideological functions within capitalism and patriarchy. Sometimes solutions are seen in simplistic terms, i.e. smashing the family and replacing it by another ideal type. However, action has to take place in the present and the actors themselves also suffer from the symptoms of oppression and repression they seek to eliminate in alternative living situations. There is a tendency to minimise the work which has to be undertaken within the self to achieve changes, and the amount of time this requires.[1] Theoretical presentations of alternatives which offer immediate relief from sexual, adult or capitalistic repression hold up a hope of utopia which is bound to fade in disillusion.[2] Like a revolution in the economic structure, person change is based upon solid work and commitment over lengthy periods of time, not upon utopian statements of ideals based on an intellectualised approach. Social workers should be particularly aware of how arduous and painful change in the self is, even when there is the desire and support is available. A revolution in the sense of personal liberation is no different, and consciousness-raising, wherever it takes place, will not produce rapid results because there is no crash course.

The process of personal liberation has to be set within a wider context than an individual seeking self-fulfilment for its own sake, often at the expense of other more basic issues. Consciousness-raising 'is not only for a psychological, individual process, but also a social process, starting from reality itself, i.e. from the world in which men live.[3] Locating the work within the framework of society and culture recognises that, to be effective, changes have to take place in these structures[4] and have a broader base than the isolated searches of a few individuals in privileged positions. The objective is the active engagement of those experiencing oppression in the continuing task of redefining and reformulating that experience. In seeking to link person change and alternative patterns of living with cultural change, a central issue is that there is no inevitable alliance between those who have rejected traditional goals and life-styles and those denied access to them. Reactions of each to the other can be as violent and exploitative as those of the dominant society.[5] Left-wing social workers may well have to choose either to use their energies to support and develop alternative life-styles and relationships which, in the current situation, will be the prerogative of a particular class, or to focus on issues which emerge directly from working-class groups where the beginning point may be the search for an adequate material base, not a rejection of one that has been achieved. This does not mean that one is irrelevant to the other, or that, where possible, links between them should not be sought. Though the contribution of social work as a profession is strictly limited at present, it is possible for individuals committed to a belief in the capacity of people to undertake this work for themselves to support its beginnings, even though they represent isolated and, to a large extent, unconnected efforts.

Those presenting predetermined solutions for others whose social and economic situation is vulnerable, but are themselves not prepared from their own position of comparative comfort to take risks, are simply perpetuating the distance between themselves and the experience of their clients. There is, moreover, no way of knowing today what pattern of relationships will emerge in a liberated society.[6] It is necessary to find our way through the problems of this one, and that cannot be accomplished by imposing solutions which either distort experience to fit the shape of the stable nuclear family and the hererosexual ideal or which deny the validity of any life within them. Although left-wing radicals would regard a change in the economic base as a precondition for the establishment of personal liberation, the position of women, for instance, in most existing socialist societies shows that one does not inevitably follow upon the other: all will not be solved at this point even though the foundation is laid. While the conditions for personal liberation cannot emerge within capitalism, the present task is to acquire experience which can be used fully later.[7]

Social work and 'openness'

Individual social workers committed to and involved in the task of accumulating experience will contribute to this process; they can relearn how to use and develop their understanding of relationships in a context of change. The task is, however, one in which distance or assumed superiority in functioning cannot be maintained. They will become as vulnerable as anyone else, their skills, experiences and weaknesses have to be pooled with others and the analysis of experience is a group, not an individual, activity. Whether any of this developing experience can be drawn into social work will depend on how much it is prepared to learn from groups of lay people whose activities challenge dearly held tenets and the theories on which they are based. It will also depend on how far social workers whose personal lives in traditional terms must to some extent be considered 'deviant' or 'disturbed' can be encouraged and are able to share with their colleagues what they have learned — the negatives as well as the positives. A judgment has to be made by social workers in this position as to how much room there is for movement in their own particular agency as well as in the profession as a whole. Since the primary task is the accumulation of experience, there seems little sense in personal exposure that will end in premature expulsion, unless this is a deliberate decision taken on either personal or political grounds.

With a liberal tradition, pride has been taken in openness as a stance of the profession and an attitude to be sought in its members. This could potentially contribute to broadening ideas on relationship patterns for children and adults, together with an increasing recognition that the stable nuclear family is not the only valid model. Openness does not require a simplistic substitution of one ideal for another, but rather an acceptance that in contemporary Britain there is no pattern which by its innate design can avoid either the contradictions it will have to face in a pre-revolutionary situation or the problems encountered in any human relationships, even though the specific nature of those problems may differ.

Although experience is being accumulated outside social work in non-nuclear family living, little is written up which includes children in a full sense. Recognition of a range of models for adult-adult and child-adult relationships is a condition many radicals would at present seek, but most experience has been accumulated in the first area. Social work itself could contribute by more research into the potential within the residential and day-care situation which does not take as its beginning an assumption of innate deficiency, but documents existing positives and achievements and looks at potential. It is not sufficient to have detailed the strengths of the nuclear family and to have written in the main about the negatives of the experience for adults and children in the residential or day-care setting. Affirming that there exist and always have existed a range of situations coming under the general heading of family is a practical beginning for social work. Equally important is a public recognition that there are legitimate and valuable experiences for adults in relationships where no children are present, whether these are homosexual or heterosexual,[8] and to try to avoid a new hierarchy being established which perpetuates the competition between relationship patterns and the sexual preferences of those within them.

Diversity is not chaos

Existing family structures within which children live are by no means identical with the simple nuclear model, nor are they to be crudely equated with the chaotic experiences which are the fate of some social workers' clients. A viable family group can consist of a parent or parents and child or children, or of a group of adults and children who have strong ties to each other which may or may not be based on blood. Structures can be complex because of divorce, separation, foster or adoptive care; in consequence, the child and adults may have lived in more than one family group. The members of the first may be present in part or totally absent from the second; all will have to cope with the emotional presence of absent persons and the problems of including new members. Although these situations have negatives in them for children and adults, the same is equally true of the current ideal, the stable nuclear family. It is only when a variety of models are legitimated in our thinking that it becomes possible to analyse the strengths and weaknesses of each instead of placing them in opposition, or to examine what external supports are required and what internal ways through the problems encountered by the adults and children within them are available.[9] At present the stress on deviation from the norm leads frequently to a devaluation not only of the model but of the life experience and identity of those within it. How can a positive view of self be achieved when parents on their own, for example, carry the burden for the establishment of what is socially termed a 'broken home', a broken experience for their children? The under-estimation of these living situations is accompanied by an under-estimation of the negatives of living within the strictly nuclear model, even though these are well documented in literature and in the experience of practitioners. There is cultural permission to express difficulties in relationships with parents or partners when the situation conforms to the norm, whereas similar feelings expressed by those living outside it are sometimes taken as a direct result of that particular pattern and a sign of its inevitable failure. Problems are too easily seen as intrinsic to the model rather than as generic to situations in which children and adults live together, and which sometimes take extreme forms.

Explorations of how dominant ideology affects the lives and identity of persons are important steps in the process of finding ways of validating the experience of those who do not conform. The ability to doubt, to share those doubts and to structure them is the beginning of reformulating and redefining relationships both within the nuclear family and in alternatives in addition to it. Social workers have been and are members of families, and they, like many others, often have a blunted capacity to doubt the nuclear family's ability to promote mental health and mature adults. Like anyone else they can cling to it unquestioningly or are revolted by it because their own mental health and individual maturity is at stake. Each person and in particular those who work closely with and in families need to have an opportunity to 'sum up the past'. Without this they inevitably remain within the net of their own internal family, whatever moves they make, because from childhood to adulthood they have not gone through the painful process of learning to be alone.[10] Their practice is inevitably affected.

It is ironic that, although committed to the development and maintenance of individuality, teaching about human growth and development has tended to neglect the issues raised by the fact that the human social animal has to learn to *be* alone. Teaching on normal development seems to focus on the smooth movement of the child from one family to becoming an adult member of yet another; a step from one womb to another with only the adolescent's rebellion intervening. Being alone is then seen primarily as a phenomenon of old age, loss through bereavement or separation rather than as a regular feature of living. A distinction has to be made between the regular, and not necessarily negative, emotional experience of being alone and separate in an essentially collective situation, and physical separation from people. Case work with individuals has offered, and can continue to offer, opportunities to learn to be alone through encouraging people to explore how they experience internal and external events. But the objective is sometimes seen as the unreserved re-establishment of full communication, for example between children and parents, husband and wife, rather than the more complex task of allowing a person to achieve and cope with the re-occurring experience of being alone as well as their connectedness with others.[11]

Significant persons

Implicit in the failure to examine the negatives of the nuclear family is
a neglect to analyse in depth the caring contributions made by members
other than the mother,[12] or to recognise the parenting element in
relationships with significant adults or children outside the nuclear
family.[13] This failure is particularly worrying when care is taking place
predominantly outside the family and in collective or group situations.
It is not hard to subscribe to the principle of Anna Freud and her
colleagues that 'Only a child who has at least one person whom he can
love, and who also feels loved and wanted by that person will develop
a healthy self-esteem,'[14] but there is no reason why the nuclear family
should be the only structure in which this type of reciprocal love is
possible. We need not only more descriptions of successes in open
fostering placements, but of those achieved outside them in extended
and complex family structures and in collective situations, including
residential care. The problem is that parenting behaviour outside the
nuclear family has not been legitimated in our thinking and in
consequence is sometimes taking place in situations where there is no
recognition or acceptance of the task involved.[15]

   The polarisation of the provision of services and parental
responsibility is symptomatic of an under-estimation of the
dependence of the nuclear family on resources outside its own narrow
boundaries. The contemporary rich family supplements what is not
available within it or locally by buying access on the private market
and spends some time transporting its children to this end. The poor
family is dependent on what is publicly provided locally or what they
can obtain through collective action. The same inevitable dependence
on supplementary relationships and resources, is, however, seen
differently; one is viewed as the responsible parent enhancing the lives
of his or her children, while the poor who seek similar ends are
considered to be avoiding their responsibilities as parents. The real
debate is not about whether supplementary or complementary
resources outside the family are necessary, but whether access to them
is to be determined by the ability to buy them, who controls them —
the private market, statutory or voluntary bodies, or the users — and
who decides what they are to be. Another facet of the exclusion of
extra-familial caring from the main model is whether community or
collective caring is possible when this is dependent on the existence *in*
people of a caring responsibility for others outside the family. Intensive
relationships within the nuclear family militate against the
preparedness of people to accept caring responsibilities beyond it. The
end-result is that 'the mother and sister or father and brother you
sensually cannot have are also the only people you are supposed to

love.'[16] Juliet Mitchell considers this to be the particular problem which has to be resolved in the unconscious of children in the nuclear family, but it also has effects in the external society. The nuclear family, like a limited company, has a limited liability.

Complementary caring

Within the nuclear family the acceptance of Talcott Parsons's strict separation of the expressive and instrumental functions, with the allocation of the former to mothers and the latter to fathers, has tended to create a belief in the inevitability of this distribution within actual families. It has been taken as a sign both of correctness and maturity, and the limitations of the model have not always been analysed. This is in marked contrast to Winnicott who, in 1968, used the term 'good enough mothering' to describe not the sex of the person but the nature of the activity.[17] Talcott Parsons's model may be useful as a basis, but applied in a simplistic way to actual situations it leads to a failure to perceive the variety that exists now. The reliance on one of these patterns may have been socially and economically necessary for a particular period, but this does not mean that it is either ideal or will remain a permanent historical feature. There is a need for more examination of families where expressive and instrumental behaviour is not distributed in a rigid or sex-typed way.[18]

Specialisation by sex, combined with the confinement of nurturing and parenting behaviour within the nuclear family, can lead to other significant figures in the child's daily life being seen as being in competition with the family, rather than supplementing or complementing care and stimulation provided within the family. The word 'substitute' is often used to cover situations which range from day to permanent care, whereas at one end of the continuum, and even in certain long-term care situations, the most appropriate description is supplementary.[19] At present the distinction seems to be more a question of who provides the care than its impact in degree or length on the relationships of the child. It indicates not the nature of the experience for the child, who through locally provided care may well see more of parents, siblings and friends than if living some distance away, albeit with relatives, but whether care is provided by kin and through personal contacts or through a statutory or voluntary body. Rutter rejects the equation of physical separation with deprivation and concludes that it is the disruption of bonds and not only those with the mother which causes distress.[20] Practice must, therefore, recognise that the child, as a social being, develops, as it grows older, relationships with people outside as well as inside the family. It is not simply a question of the child being located within another nuclear family, but of a wider view of the child's pattern of relationships and a plan which takes them into account.

The language used to describe people outside the family who accept a caring function towards the child is significant. Adults with whom the child has developed a relationship are frequently awarded the title 'aunty' or 'uncle'; similarly foster care is provided by people who, if not called 'mum' and 'dad', are usually 'aunty' or 'uncle', and houseparents are often referred to in similar ways. Both general terms used to describe people providing foster and residential care include the word 'parent'.[21] Whilst this can be justified in the sense that they are relationships which are known to the children, they are at the same time indicators of an inability on the part of the individual and on the societal level to envisage genuine parenting behaviour taking place beyond the nuclear family and close kin by people who are not related to the child in this way. Both the child and adult are prevented from validating their experience or even recognising it for what it is except by replacing the parents or remaining in competition with them.

The limitations of the concept of the psychological parent

The concept of the psychological parent used by Freud, Goldstein and Solneit[22] may be useful in identifying the main bond, but their model is deceptively simple. In some situations bonds to adults in the family are more distinguished by their similarity of strength than difference; and difference does not in itself remove the positive function of a bond. On separation there is the danger that the main bond will be seen as being within a family and not with a person who has moved out, and perhaps will remain outside, of one. In the final analysis, in many cases, it is not simply a question of emotional ties, but the practicalities of providing physical care, which decide the issue. The range of possible alternatives is strictly limited by our social arrangements and provision as well as by the pressures on men to be available for work.

Because 'good enough' experience tends to be equated with parenting in a nuclear family situation, attempts are currently being made to define more closely the points at which parenting figures living outside the family can or should be excluded from any involvement in it. The most influential of these, 'Beyond the Best Interests of the Child',[23] is intended as a guide for judges and social workers who wish to make child-centred decisions. It takes as one of its main concerns the protection of the new or remaining parent from the interference of the non-custodial parent. The authors seem to imply that rather than being an exception to a general rule of developing inclusive relationships, exclusion should be the rule because intervention is seen as disruptive. But intervention by kin living outside the nuclear unit is not a new feature antipathetic to the family's existence, it is a characteristic of extended family situations[24] in Britain. Lots of people and institutions interfere with parents carrying out day-to-day care— neighbours, social workers, teachers, doctors, etc. The difference between them and the 'non-custodial parent' is that one is culturally acceptable or imposed and the other is not. Resolutions to situations cannot be enforced; they must be experienced and lived before ways through can be found. The emphasis on exclusion, moreover, represents a marked change from the previous general rule in child care that whenever possible continuity and inclusion was desirable. It is all very well to affirm that children must be rescued from the consequences of separation when families divide, but sometimes the very nature of the rescue structures the conflict in ways that prevent resolution.

Short-term imposed solutions often ignore the social complexity of the problem and its long-term dimensions. For instance, child-centredness should ultimately involve three dimensions, not one. First, there is the requirement for adequate provision for adults in the child's life to follow through 'child-centred' solutions. The current concentration of the use of the term to specific situations where children are separated from biological parents, as opposed to children remaining with them, is political, because it is difficult to envisage how its extension could be made possible within the existing society Second, a long-term dimension recognises that decisions in specific instances to exclude a person from the life of a family may appear to meet the needs of a child at a given point, not necessarily for all time. But decisions to later involve the 'non-custodial parent' will be affected by the way that person was treated earlier. Third, a child-centred approach must also be adult-centred. Continuing the example of a child separated from family, the exclusive focus on the child is not possible even here. Where it is agreed that it is necessary, either temporarily or permanently, to cut off contact between an adult and child, it is not easy to carry this through, even though the adult is in agreement with the goal. These moves are taken out of step with the culturally accepted progress from childhood to adulthood, and in many cases with the emotional time of both. A parent's capacity to tolerate this has to be recognised rather than taken for granted, and the meaning and emotional impact of the separation for them understood.[25] That there are no clear expectations of the parent of a child in care or a parent living apart from his or her child for any other reason, is witnessed by the many people who are experiencing this at present and are trying to find ways through for themselves and their children. We have to live out as well as think out the implications of moving towards a society in which, for an increasing number of people, more than one marriage relationship, whether confirmed in law or not, will become part of their life pattern, and many children will experience more than two parenting figures during their childhood. It is interesting that there seems to be an accompanying trend to approve for young children earlier contact with group experiences outside the nuclear family. We shall be impelled to take into the family new members and recognise that others exist outside or within another family. In a sense children and adults will carry within themselves a collective family, which is not the same as having a chaotic experience. The latter can exist in a stable nuclear family as well as outside this model. It is a universal feature of the family that relationships between men and women are durable,[26] it is our specific requirement that they should be lifelong.

Putting forward the principle that the child's psychological parent should be protected from interference leaves a number of issues untouched. When the psychological parent is an identified homosexual, the relationship is more likely to be denied than accepted because it is considered harmful. Similarly, it is insufficient to leave many parents free to get on with the job, because intervention and action is required both of the social worker and the parent in order to create conditions in which adequate parenting can take place. Fathers on their own have only recently gained the right to decide to remain at home and look after their children without being required to register for work. Anna Freud and her colleagues appear to deal with this problem by asserting that day-to-day caring and psychological parenthood are to be equated. The psychological parent could tend to be seen as the person who already possesses the means socially and economically. In giving the extremes of uninterrupted day-to-day care by a parent and the visiting or visited parent the authors opposed the maximum with the minimum, while many adults' and childrens' lives are less black and white than this suggests.

If severance of contact with the non-custodial parent who creates conflict is taken as a general rule for good practice rather than a necessity in extreme circumstances, it becomes an act of aggression which is less likely to be in the long-term best interests of the child than a defence of a model of the family which is already outside the experience of that particular group of adults and children. It is undeniable that conflicts occur, and that some at the moment are insoluble, not intrinsically, but because we are using psychological tools which are either inappropriate or under-developed. 'Non-custodial parent' is a legal, not a social, term. The position is not sufficiently acceptable — it is certainly recognisable — or understood to have been given a name which is neither derogatory nor which transfers it from a social to a legal context. There is a crisis in the specific social work sense of the word. Losing adults and gaining others is not a new phenomenon for the nuclear family, but while formerly they were generally removed by death, they now remove themselves and are located somewhere else. This is the source of the problem. Anna Freud is worried lest the actual physical separation of the symbolically united and powerful parent figures of the unconscious will lead to the development of children who are unable to identify with or accept adult guidance and authority.[27] One of the difficulties for the use of these ideas in social work is the potential and incorrect equation of the symbolic with the actual parent,[28] the situation encountered in practice. Moreover, there is an uncanny game played by some psychoanalysts which allows them and no one else to predict causal connections between unconscious processes, actual behaviour and changing social patterns on a general and not a specific individual level. It is obvious that the increase in the number of families where the parents are not united under one roof will affect the development of children, but it is not inevitably socially or emotionally disastrous.

A psychoanalytic approach which assumes the ideal nature of the stable nuclear model creates over-simplification, first, in implying that socialisation has to be located primarily within the family, and second, in assuming that this is mutually satisfying to the caring figures unless there is some pathological feature in the parents', and in particular the mother's, personality. Enid Balint offers a different approach by suggesting that there is no inevitable mutuality between mother and child of the type envisaged in the idea of the mother and baby as the 'nursing couple'. From this standpoint different questions emerge and it becomes important both within the family and the group situation to understand how a capacity for concern for others without mutual satisfaction becomes possible within relationships. The reference point proposed is the theory of object relations and the study is of a process which starts in the two-person relationship, but which 'needs, if it is to develop fully, a particular kind of multi-person relationship the structure of which has not been described but which deserves serious study'.[29] At a time when children's rights and needs are being elevated, or rather downgraded, to a simplistic banner cry, it is worth recording that children are not receptacles. Social workers need to retain their conviction that, except in extreme and specific circumstances, children and parents should not be polarised, that, in Enid Balint's words, we recognise 'parents and child as equally involved human beings, not thinking that only one of the partnership is human, with drives and needs . . .'[30]

Collective living

Living outside a family can be a temporary or a permanent experience, a decision imposed from outside, or by the family. More rarely it is a positive decision to explore new patterns of group living and relationships. For a substantial minority of people living outside a family involves some form of public intervention and institutional care. In some of these the issues of social control are so dominant that there is little opportunity for the development of the positive elements of group living, and if they are discovered they emerge in spite of, and not because of, the institution; in others they exist. It is likely that, apart from a few isolated examples, group living will be regarded by those who are involved in it as a poor second best to life in the nuclear family, rather than an alternative or an addition to it. The main impetus for validating collective living either as an alternative or as complementary to the nuclear family, whether on a temporary or a permanent basis, will come from groups outside social work with a variety of political and religious backgrounds, who are committed to setting up non-nuclear, non-biological units. Although it is not possible to explore it here, any analysis of the commune movement and its potential has to take into account the fact that it is not a new historical phenomenon, even though its re-emergence in the contemporary context has specific origins. Communes or experiments in collective living have a long history.[31] They have no inherent remedy for success or revolutionary potential.

For some young people the move out of the family is part of growing up, part of an identity crisis which is at once individual and collective. Erikson, in his work on adolescence, put forward the view that to understand adolescence, culture and ideology must be put alongside psychoanalytic knowledge, because there is a persistent endeavour of the generation to join together in the effort to provide a series of 'expectable environments'. Tradition has to be restructured to make sense of the constant changes in the environment. It is, therefore, interesting that he thinks 'the functioning ego, while guarding individuality, is far from isolated, for a kind of commonality links egos in mutual activation. Something in the ego process is — well identical.'[32] This dual commitment to the individual and the collective task is embodied in the commune, and in the view of some radicals its function is limited to this. The commune need in no way undermine the nuclear family as the place in which children should be cared for, it becomes a place in which the young adult can avoid isolated living or the student hostel. Reimut Reich thinks that the commune can sometimes help them 'to bear, and fight, the social and psychological pressure to which they are particularly susceptible as single people'.[33]

The allocation of this particular function to the commune of young adults is no guarantee that life there will be radical in the left-wing sense, but can represent the identification of a stage in the development in which the task is to learn to be alone, to be apart from the nuclear family before assuming commitments within a new one. It is hardly surprising that Mills found that the identity achieved in the commune — an intense awareness of self — was transitory, and that commitment to a pair relationship usually involved a withdrawal.[34] There is evidence that many of the young commune members rejoin the main society after this initial separation from it, and that there is a high turnover in membership with a regular movement back into the straight society.[35] The process of separating from the family of origin is positively encouraged by the tolerance in many communes of a wide range of behaviour, of drug use, and by the value placed on being in crisis. It is also significant that membership seems in the main to be from the middle class, and that it is in many ways at present a class privilege. From this point of view the commune fulfils a similar function to the eighteenth-century grand tour of the aristocracy; it is a complement to the university experience, a potential replacement for national service or, for those who stress its therapeutic qualities, an adjunct to the health service. Essentially at a tangent from ordinary living, a useful way is provided for coping with the problems a young adult can present in the nuclear family. No challenge to the established order of things is necessarily made, and indeed the commune can be co-opted into this order because it relieves pressure on the nuclear family. Here the commitment to collective living and the non-biological unit is reduced to a minimum; the commune is an interlude. Although there is no intention of under-estimating the importance of the experience for the individual, it is not radical in its impact on the class structure or on the ideology of the family.

A potential challenge is involved where there is an attempt to destructure in order to restructure experience.[36] Drugs are political because they are often connected with the process of questioning what is accepted. A distinction has to be made between those who use drugs essentially for a retreat into the inner self because this is the 'last vestige of individuality left to them by society',[37] and those who use drugs as part of the work sometimes described as desocialisation in order to try to encompass more fully a new order of relationships. Here the attempt is to develop a counter-culture. The latter will condemn those who depend on drugs or use mysticism in such a way that it leads to a 'quietism' which 'colludes fully with the exploitative system'.[38] This use is at one and the same time the pinnacle of individualism and a sign of its retreat. In contrast, Cooper thinks that the true mystics have always been 'intensely aware of the circumambient society and in this sense are truly political men'.[39] For Cooper, the objective of drug use is not an individual trip but a change in the basis of relationships which is complementary to working for a revolution in the economic base.

Within this framework the commune is more than a temporary life-style or an interlude, it is an ideological commitment to the development of new types of living arrangements and relationships. While most of these aim to restructure relationship patterns to either exclude, minimise or transcend the nuclear and biological dimensions, and in this sense they are radical, the analysis on which they base their objectives can range through the religious and political spectrum. Their goals can be compatible with continuing capitalism, because they are either attempts to increase the range for individual or spiritual fulfilment or to develop more comfortable patterns of relationships. For these groups of people, relationship change within their own group is sufficient in itself. Some left-wing radicals see the promises of immediate solutions, of hopes to be fulfilled today, as unrealistic objectives inevitably doomed to failure. A consequence can be that insufficient attention is given to the fact that communes have to exist within and not apart from society, whose impact exists not only in the external environment but in the communards themselves.[40] Because of this Reimut Reich thinks that imposed as opposed to spontaneous solutions are in themselves repressive, and that the repression experienced in couple relationships is not exclusive to that pattern, rather that 'in the present historical circumstances repression is a common denominator of most sexual relationships'.[41] The same strictures would apply to adult-child relationships. The commune offers no guarantee of solutions which are compatible with the aim of economic revolution or person liberation. By removing some people, in the main the middle class, from wage labour, the possibility of their survival remains dependent upon others remaining in it. There have, for instance, been bitter complaints that commune life, particularly the rural commune, is yet another of those experiences which can only be attained through access to or the possession of private wealth.[42] Far from offering an alternative society, it could be an additional class privilege which continues to ensure that members of the middle and upper classes receive the greatest gain, in this case from economic and social co-operation. While it remains a class privilege its revolutionary potential is minimal.

Radical changes in actual behaviour towards women and parenting in no way inevitably follow from life in the commune. One American author found that in the communes his research team visited women were not counted in the membership; they were appendages to the group, the 'chicks'. Rigby, in a British study, reported that in spite of efforts in one commune to break down the sex allocation of functions, the members were aware that the female parents of children continued to take the main responsibility for their care, and biological fathers spent more time with their children than other commune members.[43] The German Kommune 2[44] is one of the few[45] to have attempted to analyse and share the issues raised in collective living for children and adults. Most other studies known to the writer mention that children exist, but their impact on commune life is glossed over. This may be because the research is deliberately adult-centred or those involved in it are unable to see the validity of collective living or its positives for children, either on the social or emotional level, and so do not raise the questions. It is significant that in Kommune 2 it was from an awareness of themselves, through a form of group therapy, of their strengths and weaknesses and of their own childhood experiences, that the seven adults in the group began to be able to respond emotionally as well as intellectually to other people's children. Originally the members had not been unanimous in their wish to take in the two children, but as the adults became more understanding of themselves and each other the children moved from being peripheral—each person wishing to spend only a limited amount of time with them—to a central position in commune life. Ultimately this spread outside the commune to other children and their parents. Their experience seems to confirm that a concept of child-centredness has to take into account at the same time a need for adult-centredness in relation to the adults in the child's life. In the absence of this dimension child-centredness becomes a crude mechanism for remedying the effects on child-adult relationships of a society where the dominant force is competition, profit-making and consumption.

Without an awareness and the development of an ability to deal with the impact of communal living, it can become as oppressive as the nuclear family, and replicate, not eradicate, the oppression of women and children. Rigby concluded that the conflict areas of communards were the desire for close personal relationships and to be apart. While many communes have a separate room for each person, a low level of participation was not accepted.[46] Jealousy and envy exist in the commune and make it like the nuclear family, 'a dangerous business because the problem can lead to breakdown or breakthrough'.[47] Another conflict area is that where the objective is the liberation of adults through a progressive destructuring of time and personality, this is to some degree incompatible with the needs of children who, in consequence, experience the freedom to be neglected rather than liberated. Kommune 2 concluded that:

we could yield only partially to our regressive desires, but never as a whole collective or for an extended length of time because of the objective reality of our political intentions in the one case and of the children in the other cases.[48]

There are no easy answers to the problem of providing sufficient security and continuity in relationships for children. In this communes are similar to the nuclear family. Communes, like nuclear family members, separate and the reasons for forming and ending a commune can be centred solely on adults', not children's, needs or wishes. Significant relationships made with children will have extended beyond the biological parents, but at crisis points it is often to them and in particular the mother that are handed back all the responsibilities placed upon them in the straight society: finding different accommodation or coping with the setting up of new day-care arrangements can be left to the biological parent. On the emotional side they can be left to cope alone with the children's reactions to these changes and to the loss or weakening of important relationships. Many adults have not learned how to maintain relationships with children at a geographical distance as opposed to group living situations where interaction on some level is inevitable, and where the children themselves can initiate and reinforce relationships.

These are problems which are generic to situations in which children and adults live together. They are not new, nor are they worse in the commune situation than they are in the nuclear family, though they may be experienced differently. The commune offers the hope that over time the problems can be identified and ways found through them by those committed to the work of forming new relationships and to the exploration of the issues raised in these collective living situations. It is important also to explore the strengths they can offer people, either at certain points in their life — the task of separation from a nuclear family is not confined to the young adult — or as permanent alternative life situations which exist in addition to the nuclear family. Idealisation of commune life will lead to its negatives being unexplored, instead of analysed and ways through sought. For instance, a danger for children experiencing a failed commune is that they will have had so many contacts that they will be unable to take part in caring relationships. They simply become the opposite of the failed nuclear family product who cares little for those beyond the confines of its walls.

Conclusion

A social worker with a commitment to the development of a range of living patterns for children and adults can offer people an opportunity, albeit often limited, to sum up and redefine their experience and identity. But this requires of social workers the ability to doubt both themselves and the dominant ideology, to genuinely explore with another person, or group of persons, ways through from one life situation into another which take into account others, whether they are children or adults. In the agencies it requires the allocation of time for this sort of work. The identification of the ground to be covered and the analysis of it is best undertaken by those on the 'inside' who are traditionally called the clients, but who actually include a number of social workers. It is only at a second stage, when the range of the paths and the validity of the journey have been established, that other outsiders can begin to participate in identifying how their particular range of skills and their access to resources can be used. In this social work is again a reactor and not a leader.

5

Biological destiny or mind-forged manacles

Introduction

At the centre of the nuclear family is the 'natural' division between the sexes of gender characteristics and of labour. Traditionally, men and women are seen as divided by their biology and tasks, consequently, for a considerable number, this entails geographical separation for the duration of the working period.[1] Unity is achieved through heterosexuality. Far from being inevitable or biologically determined, a cursory reading of anthropological literature demonstrates that divisions based on sex exist in all human societies, but that there is a wide variety of viable patterns for the allocation of gender characteristics and tasks. Equally important, they indicate that although men and women work collaboratively, some degree of conflict exists between them.[2] The validation of one pattern in a culture at a specific historical period is often considered to have as its sole foundation the limits of human biology and psychology, but ideas about the nature of masculine and feminine behaviour and of sexuality have also to be located in our own culture and its socio-economic structure.

Social work teaching seems to concentrate mainly on two areas. First, on studies of other cultures, usually pre-industrial and less complex than our own. Here the problem for the practitioners is that they work in an advanced industrial society where expectations of men and women are in the process of changing at least marginally, and even given a fairly static pattern the degree to which the ideal can be achieved varies with social class. A large part of social work is concerned with working-class people, and situations which are exceptions to the rule, for example the family where the mother or father is not present, the physically or mentally handicapped mother-wife or father-husband who cannot meet expectations, the elderly man or woman who is having to learn to undertake tasks previously carried out by a partner now dead, or the single person who has always, or periodically, been in this position.

Although literature about other cultures is used to demonstrate patterns radically different from our own, it can at the same time leave an impression that expectations are rigidly observed in each society except by those who are socially or psychologically maladjusted. In reality most cultures allow for variations in the way tasks are allocated when the 'logic of the situation demands it'. Men and women can, in these instances, undertake tasks usually performed by the other sex.[3] Because of the nature of their work, social workers need not only to understand the way one cultural pattern differs from another at a point in time, and the range of the variations possible, but also when deviation in one of them can be expected because the situation faced by the man or woman is atypical. They have to consider what adaptations are made to allow this to happen, how this affects the person and those around him or her. An understanding that these mechanisms exist and always have existed in our own society is important for even the most traditionally oriented social worker. Moreover, members of ethnic minority groups will begin from a different base from our own and social workers now need to know what they are, and to understand their impact on each other at points of interchange with our own cultural patterns.

Second, within our own culture social work teaching, as opposed to social administration and sociology, concentrates primarily on aspects of theories about masculinity and femininity. The objective seems to be to clarify the nature and genesis of the characteristics of a mother-wife and husband-father-worker.[4] Implicit in this exploration is, in the main, the equation of mature sexuality with a heterosexual preference, of mature femininity with motherhood within marriage. In a very real sense women as persons do not exist in social work literature, but in this it simply reflects the culture and the problems of the contributing disciplines. Concentrating on clarifying the application of particular aspects of theories will produce relevant guidelines for practice only when there is a general acceptance of the theory as a whole, and relative stability in the cultural value placed on maintaining a particular pattern. But patterns have changed in the past[5] and there are clear signs that, as traditionally conceived, the divisions based on sex are no longer socially useful. Theoretical work other than that produced by women and gay liberationists is contributing to the doubt. Very early it becomes clear from sources that controversy exists and that the available theoretical tools are inadequate. One of the aims of women's studies[6] is to remedy this defect. The issue is not simply one of academic purity; it crucially affects relationships, actions and the life situations of people with whom social workers come into daily contact, and the expectations social workers have of them. Male or female, heterosexual or homosexual, it is becoming increasingly difficult to constrain people to fit the models traditionally prescribed for them. At present the observer, 'the knower' who finds herself/ himself faced with this problem has two main options: the subject observed can be seen as deviant or disturbed, or some change in the model used and the values attached to it must occur.[7]

Mature masculinity and femininity are frequently presented as polarities. One is characterised by being logical, rational, emotionally controlled, competitive and aggressive while the other embodies feeling, dependence, intuition and passivity, with the ultimate form found only in marriage and motherhood. There are warnings for those striving against this definition of themselves: the women, for instance, may acquire a stricter super-ego than their more feminine counterparts, but they do so at the cost of repressing their dependent needs.[8] Bettleheim considers the fulfilment of womanhood is co-incidental with being a mother and the companion of a man.[9] For another writer the acceptance by women that they are 'nurturance' is the path both to their own mental health and the way to 'attain the goal of a good life and a secure world in which to live it'.[10]

It is ironic that therapists identify characteristics as feminine and at the same time see them as less mature than those they ascribe to men. Within this scheme of things women are by definition neurotic.[11] Whether male or female, those who do not conform by design or accident cannot escape the contradiction; they become women with masculine traits or, alternatively, men with feminine traits. The term is not used in a specific, psychoanalytic sense, it is socially derogatory. If their 'deviance' is attached to a cause they are seen to have simply translated their neurotic symptoms. The cause may well be thought more productive than lying in bed with a tension headache, but it remains 'its neurotic equivalent'.[12]

In discussing theory it becomes vital to identify when moves from description to prescription occur and to recognise that those who appeal to the absolutes of biology and psychology are not supported by many within those disciplines. Prescriptions come from ideology, from what is valued and valuable in a specific society. The variations between societies are vast. Within our own, individual and group variations are considerable. The academic disciplines which impinge on this area can point to the structure within which change takes place at a specific point in our history, but the limits we identify within this structure are not those of human potential. Those who argue that the development of new relationship patterns between men and women creates stress are making an incontrovertible point. The argument assumes that no, or far fewer, conflicts exist for people living within the normative expectations, and that therefore less stress is experienced by those trying to conform than by those who do not. There are at least two flaws in this approach. The first is that ideals for male-female behaviour have to cover a wide variety of life situations and contain conflicting expectations. Stress is experienced because a person has to resolve these conflicts. Second, social norms are not static, they change. Social historians and sociologists have, for instance, traced the effects of industrialisation on the social ideals for men and women. Human relationships cannot be isolated from the effects of changes currently taking place, and again some stress is inevitable. Whether more or less experienced by those responding to these changes or those resisting them, and what class dimensions are involved, is for debate.[13]

The point is significant for social workers because they meet men and women not in the mass or in theoretical abstractions but in their human diversity. Where stereotypes for behaviour are used as guidelines, as opposed to an awareness of the range of potential ways of responding, little account can be taken of variables. Where the impression is created that stress is mainly experienced by men and women who deviate in some way, there is a tendency to respond to this group over-readily, accompanied by a failure to recognise its existence when there is conformity or simply to consider the person immature or poorly adjusted to their role. The predilection for the idea of role, with its stress on the need for order and conformity in social behaviour, may be an attempt to resolve a theoretical problem for sociologists,[14] but it negates what social work stands for — a recognition of the unique aspects of a person's experience and responses in social situations.

The biological base

Basic data on anatomical differences is well known. Less emphasis is placed upon other biological differences and similarities between men and women. These are, however, well documented in readily available literature and reference should be made to these sources.[15] Contention arises not from the data, but from the interpretation of its implications. There is now sufficient evidence to question the conception of the great divide between male and female, and this needs moving into social work. For instance, all men and women carry within their bodies the vestiges of the genitals of the other; the vagina is not a passive receptacle of the active male organ,[16] and, whatever the nature of women's unconscious, their conscious sexual behaviour involves activity and initiation. Equally important is the recognition that however clearly differences in the musculature and in the distribution of the sex hormone testosterone are identified, it is undisputed that although biologically 'women as a group tend to cluster in a different way from men . . . individual men and women show substantial overlap'.[17]

The black and white has already incorporated a grey area. Those who claim that nature has set great store on sexual dimorphism,[18] i.e. the two distinct forms of male and female, are not helped by studies which are constantly testing the assumed boundaries set by human biology. It is remarkable that great emphasis is placed on the limits determined by the sex of a person, whereas the fact that human beings are neither equipped by their biology for life under water nor in the air has in no way prevented the validation of the search to find ways of enabling human beings to fly, to live for long periods in submarines or in space. The line between life and death is no longer clear, and the division between one human body and another has been blurred by transplant operations. Biological fact is acted upon by technology and culture, and while in some areas we scream biological determinism, in others we stress and applaud human adaptability. It is ironic that although for centuries we have sought to emphasise what makes man different from the animals, in an attempt to assert the naturalness of the divisions between the sexes there is now a search to 'regain their instinctual animal nature and forget what man has made of man'.[19]

On closer view, animal studies challenge simple polarisations based on sex. Findings, it is true, tend to confirm an overall male dominance in the higher animals, but as an isolated fact this ignores the existence of female hierarchies which also exist in complex relationship with those of the males. The argument that greater quantities of the hormone testosterone found in males is directly responsible for male dominance in man and the animals[20] fails to take into account examples of primates where, despite this, the female is more aggressive, competitive and dominant than the male.[21] It seems that the significance for social behaviour of the hormones is not clear.[22] That the female carries the reproductive function does not mean that biology determines that she also nurtures, either among the animals or in humans.[23] Parenting behaviour in humans is measured by social indices; so far the connections established have been with social class, not with the correct distribution of sex hormones. Animal studies do serve a limited value, but their 'function can be no more than to show some of the extent examples of diverse sex role behaviour'.[24]

Biology, in many discussions, serves a convenience function: when it illustrates what is considered to be desirable 'normal' male or female behaviour it is affirmed as a limit set on human development, but it is either ignored when it does not, or the different behaviour is seen as the result of human evolution. Thus, homosexuality can be regarded as unnatural although animal studies confirm that homosexual attachments are found in all species, and it can be asserted to be an illness, even though more likely to occur among identical than fraternal twins.[25]

The fact that women's anatomical destiny is acted upon by technology and culture is often omitted. The expression of sexuality has always left room for sex which is neither reproductive nor part of an intimate relationship, but in the past these have been legitimated in the main as male activities.[26] Now adequate birth control methods have clearly offered these possibilities to women. Abortion and sterilisation are confirmations of this fact. A woman can live a sexually active life and never become a mother, she need experience menstruation only occasionally or for fifteen minutes a month.[27] The mark of womanhood and the fall of Eve can become a minor physical event. In 1958 Titmuss pointed to the social revolution that has occurred for women through the reduction in the amount of time spent in bearing and rearing children.[28] This, combined with the assertion that women are people, not simply some one's wife or mother or sex object, has led to a broadening of focus from reproductive woman or woman as object to female sexuality. Research mainly by Kinsey, and Masters and Johnson[29] challenges the view of woman's experience of genital sex as a passive and somewhat insensitive receptacle awaiting stimulation by the thrusting active male. Although women are incapable of the genital rape of a male, all else is not determined by this. The physical responses of male and female during intercourse and orgasm are similar whether the latter is a result of intercourse, masturbation or fantasy. While the desire for vaginal penetration is necessary for heterosexual genital sex and for reproduction there is no physiological difference between an orgasm which results from vaginal penetration as opposed to clitoral stimulation.[30]

Within the women's movement the denial of women's sexuality and the accompanying emphasis on the vaginal orgasm, an orgasm which does not exist as a separate, superior entity, as mature female sexuality has political implications. The conclusion is that it is necessary to redefine women's sexuality because at present it is seen as what pleases men.[31] The significance of this view spreads beyond heterosexual relationships. First, sexual satisfaction does not require relationships with a male, and second, sexual pleasure is obtainable either from men *or* women, thus heterosexuality becomes not an absolute but an option. The whole question of human sexual relationships is extended beyond the confines of the present male-female role system.[32] It is in the light of this view of sexuality that statements like 'lesbianism, like male homosexuality, is a category of behaviour possible only in a sexist society'[33] must be understood. The argument moves from describing the range of physical responses to the actual and potential experience of physically and emotionally satisfying relationships with people of the same sex.

As soon as biological data is translated into social behaviour the question of the meaning given to it and the value placed upon it arises.[34] Clearly, there is a significant difference between what is thought socially to be 'natural' and 'normal' and the physiological sexual reactions in the male and female.[35] It is also quite inaccurate to place the challenge to these traditional expectations solely at the door of the liberation movement, because it comes from the science itself.

Greater precision and sophistication in ways of studying sexual behaviour has resulted in biologists no longer thinking in absolute terms of 'male' and 'female'. To some it may appear as if the picture has become altogether too blurred, but to others it seems we may be replacing the old stereotyped concepts with others somewhat nearer the biological truth.[36]

There is in addition a move away from the emphasis on the limits set on human beings by their biology towards an insistence that 'Creation is an ongoing process, within which man has potentialities so far untapped and explored only to a limited extent. In an important sense, man is not an end but a way.'[37] This contrasts with the image of masculinity and femininity presented to many social workers. A recent survey of the literature used on courses shows that very low priority was given to literature questioning traditional beliefs about women.[38] It is ironic that, while committed to enabling individuals to achieve their potential, social workers are offered theories of woman who is determined by her biology and psychology — woman's beginning is also her end, because she has nowhere else to go.

Psychoanalysis

In her book 'Psychoanalysis and Feminism'[39] Juliet Mitchell makes an important contribution to the debate. Much of the previous discussion in the women's movement had concentrated on the economic and social oppression of women. Though recognising these as important factors, she sees the origins of women's oppression as being in the 'head and heart as well as in the home'.[40] For her 'in the head' refers not simply to the processes of socialisation,[41] but to the way in which men and women find their place in human society, the way we acquire in our unconscious the patriarchal culture. Though incomplete and inadequate, she thinks Freudian psychoanalytic theory offers a base from which development can take place.[42] Psychoanalytic theory, as commonly taught to social workers, is contaminated by ideological prescriptions and it becomes necessary to preface discussions by outlining its intended limits. First, psychoanalysis[43] is concerned with the development of theories about unconscious, and not conscious, behaviour. Second, it is descriptive and analytic, and is not, or was not, intended to be prescriptive either in its models of man or woman or patterns of sexuality. If it has become the latter in the hands of some analysts and social workers this is a distortion. Third, the use of the theory and practice of psychoanalysis for adapting people's behaviour was firmly rejected by Freud.[44] Fourth, terms are used in a specific sense. 'Feminine' describes what is passive and weak, and 'masculine' what is active and strong. Their originator thought that it was obvious that this was an 'inadequate empirical and conventional equation'.[45] Moreover, although biological differences are reflected in mental life, 'no individual is limited to the modes or reaction of a single sex but always finds some room for those of the opposite one'.[46]

This important qualification is often lost in social work teaching because of the problem of trying to condense complex and controversial theories into comparatively few lectures. Eclectic teaching all too frequently produces an apparent convergence of all disciplines towards one point of agreement: that of social convention. The theory is so reduced that the dynamic of the discipline is lost. There is often little distinction between theories which relate to social conscious and unconscious behaviour. Terms which are used in a specific psychoanalytic sense are broadened to take in common usage with all its accompanying confusions. Mature womanhood is the maternal figure who withdraws from the world of activity to re-emerge only when her children have left home. The immature woman clings to her old sense of self and to her career; the immature man is the one who wishes to become more than 'an auxiliary mother who can take over in emergencies'.[47] By this time the model becomes, in spite of minor concessions, prescriptive and conveniently coincides with the needs of our particular socio-economic structure. Similarly, except as an immature, abnormal or less satisfactory expression of sexuality, adult homosexuality is rarely discussed.[48] Homosexuality challenges the traditional definition of mature adult men and women, and the neat ordering of personal relationships into roles. It is particularly worrying that although about one in twenty of the population are homosexual, many social workers can refer only to theory which sees people with this sexual preference as abnormal or as a continuation of what should be an adolescent episode.[49]

One of the contributions of psychoanalysis is identifying masculinity, feminity and sexuality as complex. Here the theory of bisexuality is significant. Freud postulates not different sources of male and female sexuality in the very young child but 'polymorphous perverse sexuality'. The human infant does not discover its sexuality and move in a regulated, chronological sequence along a path towards genital heterosexual activity, passing neatly and completely through the oral and anal stages; it is more a question of there being 'nothing to stop the multifarious and multitudinous aspects of the drive that comprises sexuality from going off in any direction wished for. Any irregularity can occur in the absence of the restraining might of the cultural inhibitions of shame, disgust and morality.'[50] Moreover, 'normal' sexuality retains some elements of these perverse impulses.[51] Repression and sublimation will not make them all disappear either from our own or our clients lives.[52]

Homosexual behaviour, at least in Freud's view, was not by implication inherently neurotic. He gives an example in 'A Case of Female Homosexuality' of an un-neurotic resolution of female sexuality in lesbianism.[53] Again, in a letter Freud wrote, 'Homosexuality is assuredly not an advantage, but it is nothing to be ashamed of, no vice, no degradation, it cannot be classified as an illness, we consider it to be a variation of the sexual function.'[54] This is far removed from the social and psychological pathology allocated to all homosexuals by some who consider acts between males (much less is written about women) as 'total fantasy without relevance of the other except as a device ... There is no reality awareness of the partner or his feelings.'[55] Such generalisation is less likely to be the product of science than of prejudice.

The care with which Freud separated the biological and the social from the psychoanalytic has not been entirely lost in post-Freudian writings, even though in the main they have been concerned with prescribing one or another sort of normality of ideal.[56] A paper by D.W. Winnicott, much less discussed among social workers than his work on primary maternal preoccupation, continued to reaffirm the position adopted by Freud and attempted to develop it. He reiterates dissatisfaction with terms but comments, 'I shall continue to use this terminology (male and female elements) for the time being since I know of no other suitable descriptive terms.'[57] He is quite clear that when he uses the words 'male' and 'female' he is not referring to persons, but to 'distilled male and female elements'[58] which are present in people irrespective of whether they are men or women. Winnicott is careful to avoid the slide from producing hypotheses about how unconscious life is experienced to discussions of conscious life or of prescribing models for male or female behaviour. Attempts to assess normality in relation to the male-female elements, Winnicott warns, depend on the social expectations of any one social group at a particular time.

> Could it not be said that at the patriarchal extreme of society sexual intercourse is rape, and at the matriarchal extreme the man with the split-off element who must satisfy many women is at a premium even if in doing so he annihilates himself.[59]

Given the nature of their work it is difficult to see how social workers can avoid importing prescriptions into the psychoanalytic theory to which they refer. Though much further removed from the arena of social action, psychoanalysts have been frequently accused by their women and gay patients of stereotyping.[60] Social workers have to be aware that in the majority of instances the application of psychoanalytic theories in the content of their clients' social relationships represents a move from their original use.

> Freud never concerned himself with the adaptation of his patients to the society of his time; he enabled them to solve their problems themselves and their relationship to their milieu was one of them — no more and no less, for example than the marital relationship, one he did not treat at all on a realistic plane as a counsellor would have.[61]

A minimum requirement of the social worker is to become aware of his or her own attitudes and biases in relation to men, women, and sexuality[62] as a necessary precondition for relationship work with clients. The suggestion is not just a moral exhortation, but has application in work with all clients, and in particular with people who are in situations which do not conform with traditional ideas about male-female activities or behaviour. Social workers who have not done this work within themselves can be of little help to people who wish to move towards a new definition, or who want to resist one. They will tend to try to impose either the traditional model or an alternative upon the life experience of clients rather than exploring the issues raised in that person's situation. In the desire to confirm our own particular compromise, there is the danger that a personal solution is confused with an absolute. Instead of seeking to co-operate with clients in the process of identifying and developing a range of solutions, competition is reaffirmed and a new hierarchy simply replaces the old one. For instance, if remaining childless is seen by the social worker as the solution for women in the current situation, there is little chance of communicating with women with children. Irrespective of what that person would do if she 'began again', the time for that sort of decision-making has gone, her context is a different one, as are the issues raised and the pressures experienced.

The social context

The uncertainty of biology and psychoanalysis is mirrored in those disciplines concerned with the study of society. In part this results from the recognition of differences within a specific society, in part because of a knowledge of other societies and cultures. Again, the doubts are all too often lost in the theory offered to social workers. While many have been introduced to an initial knowledge of cross-cultural studies, these often serve to demonstrate only separateness and absolute differences between human cultures rather than their continuity. They become fascinating representations of an inferior past or deviations from the ideal rather than valid variations. This view has been derived partly from the fact that, until recently, comparative data was more available for pre-industrial than for other industrial societies. In addition, there is often a failure to distinguish between the term 'sex' and 'gender'. Anne Oakley defines sex as 'the biological differences between male and female, the visible differences in the genitalia, the related differences in the procreative function' and gender as 'being a matter of culture: it refers to the social classification "masculine" and "feminine".'[63]

The influence of social expectations and hence of adults close to the child was clearly identified before the issue was given prominence by the women's movement,[64] and the power of gender identity over the biological sex of a person has been documented in the works of John Money who has shown that the sex of social assignment or the gender identity predominates in the person's idea of their sexual identity.[65] This core of gender identity is fixed by two years of age, and while in no way proposing that the central nervous system of the human baby is either 'neuter or neutral' Stoller thinks 'we can say that the effects of these biological systems, organised prenatally in a masculine or feminine direction, are almost always (with the exception of hypogonadal males) too gentle in humans to withstand the more powerful forces of environment in human development'.[66]

The importance of passing in the gender role of choice is not under-estimated by one of the clinics specialising in surgery for transsexuals. The person is required to pass in the community for at least a year before the operation, which is followed by voice training, learning how to do hair, to sit, dress, etc. according to the social expectations of the chosen sex.[67] As Anne Oakley has pointed out, it is this gender behaviour which determines everyday social responses;

the existence of penis, clitoris, breasts are not checked.[68]

Social convention about the appropriate expression of male and female sexuality varies in the same society at different historical periods as well as between societies. Robert Burton's seventeenth-century woman lead to the plaint 'of woman's unnatural, insatiable lust what country, what village does not complain'.[69] It contrasts strangely with the Victorian decarnalised ideal for women.[70] Though submerged, devouring woman remained in folk culture and was in evidence in the music hall jokes about the fit young man who emerges as the emaciated husband after the honeymoon. A more recent version is the stereotype of the women's liberation supporter who devours and castrates all men who stand in her path.[71] The idea of woman awaiting arousal by the male leads not only to lesbianism being relatively ignored except where maternal functions are involved, but to their exclusion from the myth of the homosexual rapist, which seems to carry within it the assumption of masculine sexual aggressiveness with only its object changed. The 'victim' is not passive woman, but young boys who are as yet uncertain of their sexuality. These myths are founded in a society which is organised around heterosexuality as the only normal expression of human sexuality.[72] Clearly, people whose relationships were legally proscribed until 1967,[73] and continue to be socially and to some extent legally oppressed tend, like others in the same position, to be forced into clandestine and casual relationships. But this can no more be used as evidence of intrinsic problems than can the existence of similar relationship patterns in heterosexuals be regarded as indicators of intrinsic deficiencies in that sexual preference.

The polarisation of homosexual and heterosexual behaviour is in itself more a result of social values than actual human behaviour. Kinsey found that a six-point scale made more sense of experience. Although some people were exclusively heterosexual or homosexual in their behaviour, others in varying degrees and at different times in their lives encompassed the two orientations.[74] The homosexual, whether male or female, may present a threat, but it is to the existing social order of which the sexual order is a part. Social images of man and woman are specific to a culture and relate only marginally to biology. Great variation in expectations and ideas exist, and in a particular culture 'each sex should do not just what it is able, but only what is thought appropriate by the other'.[75]

Male and female roles

Within social work the sociological concept of role is often loosely used and little account is taken of the identified limits of the idea or the debate surrounding it. Sophistications like role fit, role reversal and role distance are taught and applied on the assumption that it is a useful idea for social workers. The theory is a tool for the analysis of functions, tasks and moral approval accorded a particular patterning of them in a specific society. Approved patterns vary between societies; in a specific society they change over time, and one of the problems in using the idea in complex industrial societies is that to assume agreement about ideal patterning for basic roles is a distortion of reality.

In contrast with social workers whose daily experience is concerned with micro-social situations where reactions are diverse, role theory speaks of the 'glass man of sociology',[76] of actors more comparable to the parts in a morality play than to the realistic theatre.[77] Generally, role theory separates out roles and only one of a person's many roles is seen to be activated at a particular time, but social workers are concerned with actual situations where the clear-cut divisions and the contained conflict of a model disintegrate.[78] In addition, in order to work, role theory has to assume agreement about definitions,[79] while empirical study[80] indicates that this is an overly simple view of life in contemporary society. A number of sociologists have been worried by the way role theory divests people of what is personal and unique to themselves in their actions and the ends they seek.[81] Goffman's concept of role distance[82] was an attempt to resolve this dilemma, but an alternative is to recognise that the severe limitations of role theory are best encountered by stepping outside, rather than amending or refining it further. Dick Atkinson considers situational analysis is a more useful sociological tool because it takes as its point of departure real persons and situations as they experience them, not ideal types or reactions. The assumption that a situation has *a* logic to it — that ascribed to it by the observer — is replaced by a recognition that there are numerous possible reactions to similar situations, different patterning for these responses and ordering of priorities. Situational analysis represents a move away from constructing theories about what people in a given culture should do, towards attempting to understand the logic and morality of what they actually do. In common with the liberation movements, there is a stress on the actual experience of persons as a basis from which to build models both at the higher and lower levels. Atkinson argues that sociological theory has tended towards consensus and determinism, and that this has caused questions to be posed in terms of how order is created and maintained in society. In contrast, he refers to Dennis Wong's work which emphasises the social, as opposed to the a-social, nature of man; the relevant question becomes how is such variety and conflict possible?[83]

A theory which takes into account complexity, variety and change comes closer to describing and analysing problems as they are encountered by social workers than one which is incapable of offering explanations of how role content is changed, new roles are introduced or relationships redefined.[84] These limitations are particularly acute in contemporary Britain. In societies which are less complex and change more slowly, theoretical analysis can produce definitions of basic roles which are fairly clear and remain valid over time. Descriptions of expectations and actual social behaviour are close enough for a bridge to exist between them which makes sense in both the world of experience and of theory, even though tensions and stresses can be seen to exist. Complex industrial society, and particularly capitalist society, is not of this order; it must by definition be changing.[85] Ideology, however, in the interests of the stability of the social order, ensures that conceptualising the impact of these changes on relationships is delayed. Behaviour which responds too quickly to changes in the economic order is regarded as anti-social, disturbed or immoral. Rapid changes in the social order are disruptive and undesirable because it takes time for them to emerge clearly and to be redefined in a way consistent with capitalism. The idea of role is useful in this slowing-down process, because definitions are inevitably based on retrospective analysis; it deals with what was agreed or appeared to be agreed. In a period of change, social work is adhering to this theory, and by translating its use from an analytic into a diagnostic tool the idea of role becomes part of a process of exhorting conformity upon people whose behaviour is more in keeping with current conditions than the cultural expectations of them.[86] Although the liberation movements have documented and analysed the oppressive nature of role definitions for certain groups, the problem is recognised beyond the radical movements. In a changing society there are periods of time during which the recognition of discrepancies between actual social conditions and cultural expectations is inexplicit, and, increasingly, sociologists are pointing to role definitions as an area in which change is required in order to maintain the existing socio-economic order.[87] Social work as part of the liberal tradition will have to take account both of the general pressures for change and specifically as these affect the expectations of men and women and sexual behaviour. In its turn this will have implications, first, for work with the family, with the institutions and people relating to it, and second, for work with persons who are women or gay.

It remains important for social workers to be acquainted with role theory in order to take ideology into account and to attempt to ensure that the theory is used in a more specific and analytic way. It is a useful gauge of the direction of change. Sex and race are both the subject of urgent social and legal attention,[88] and this in itself indicates some reassessment of these groups' social positions and the expectations of them. The importance of legal changes is demonstrated by Dahrendorf's analysis of the nature and degree of sanctions exercised over certain behaviour associated with roles. He distinguishes between:

(a) The must expectations which are the hard core of social roles and are codified by law, for instance parents must not ill-treat their children or abandon them, women must not be discriminated against on the basis of sex in certain defined situations, people must not be discriminated against on the basis of race.

(b) The shall expectations, for instance, motherhood should be within marriage, parents should remain together for life, people in parenting positions should have a heterosexual preference.

(c) The can expectations, for instance, fathers can take part in caring for their children.[89]

All these levels are subject to change over time, and interact with each other in ways which produce contradictions, not harmony for persons. Emmett, for example, is forced to conclude that role conflict is endemic in British society so that each person is left to make his own judgments about priorities.[90] Similarly, after having noted that the analysis of role assumes consensus in order to make the model work, Banton subsequently states that the notion of role is problematic because the more diffuse the content of basic roles tends to be, the less likely is there to be any agreement over core values or the content of roles.[91] This is the situation that exists in contemporary Britain.

The social worker is faced with the effects of this confusion in the lives of people and in the inadequacy of their theoretical tools. Feminine woman is seen as a wife and subsequently a mother, yet she is liberated at the level of law from specific discrimination which springs from her sex. She is to some extent freed to be a person, which inevitably sets her in conflict with the ideal mother and wife who, for a period at least, exists only in relation to the children and husband. The use of the notion of role in areas which relate to the shall and the can expectations is particularly problematic.[92] Not only is it difficult to allocate some of the expectations between the two, but conflicts exist between them. The Finer Report at one and the same time advocates the right of mothers to decide whether or not to work, and that children under the age of three years should remain with their mothers.[93] Similar demands are made by others of all mothers with under school-age children. The passage of time has even here altered from a general prescription for mothers not to work towards specifying mothers of a particular age group of children.

It is true that this lack of clarity leaves some room for individual choice,[94] but it would be mistaken to assume that there is a wide-range choice open. Limitations are imposed by the nature of society as it exists or as it is desired to be. It is predictable that while there is an attempt to remove the factors inhibiting women in the world of work there is at the same time an attempt to reinforce and more strictly define the expectations of a parent and in particular the mother.

Merton's 'role articulation' and 'status articulation'[95] remain useful ideas for social workers who have to analyse the way these conflicts are structured, the problems this creates, and where and what alternative resources are required at specific points in time. Merton uses the term 'role articulation' to describe decisions which have to be made about which of the multiple expectations facing a person in a single role is given priority. Judgments about the particular decisions result not only from the preferences of the individual, but from their effect on others. For instance, a working mother means that, given the traditional division of labour between home and work, both the children and the husband — if there is one — have a part-timer to service them.[96] Problems are seen, therefore, to arise because the woman is absent from the home and not because of the length of time a man must, or chooses to, spend at his place of work. Another factor to be taken into account is the degree of disruption caused by a decision. Because mothers are expected to be available all the time, day care is frequently seen by social workers and others as a residual service for children who are at risk rather than as a universal service necessary for parents, male or female, who go out to work.[97] They fail to identify the fact that the problems of day care do not end when a child reaches school age — the approved age for a mother to begin working — because the school hours and holidays do not coincide with those of the majority of workers.[98]

It is naive to suggest that the absence of day care has occurred solely because children's needs are seen as being most satisfactorily met by remaining at home with the mother. The separation of home from work occurred as part of a historical process and the development of the housewife role did not emerge from humanitarian reasons. Work moved out of the home, and men with it, as a result of industrialisation. The exclusion of the personal and the emotional from the work situation enabled modern capitalism to develop with great rapidity and efficiency.[99] Female labour remains available in times of labour shortages, in national emergencies, at times of high male unemployment and to supplement low wages. Day care is provided when the need for women to work coincides with national, not personal, crises or shortages.[100] Its presence or absence does not inevitably relate to what is 'good child care' or to liberating women.

Choices have to be made not only between different expectations of a person in one role (role articulation), but between the expectations and obligations attached to different roles occupied by a person (status articulation). In emergencies where conflict arises between two role sets, there is a temporary abandonment of one role. Although disruptions at the place of work are inevitable, and a person in a high status position in an organisation is likely to be absent from it at outside meetings and conferences, these are regarded as legitimate because they are the result of choices within one role set (role articulation), not between different roles as, for instance, the parent and the worker role (status articulation). The cultural expectation that women provide child care means that in conflict situations they, not the fathers, are expected to make the choice of home rather than work, and this expectation affects in turn the type of work for which they are seen as most fitted. Women's work is, therefore, frequently in jobs where one individual is most easily replaced by another.[101] There are fundamental implications for men in families where either no mother is present or she is handicapped to a degree which involves him in making frequent choices between his work and his family.[102]

Men are excluded, in the main, from participating fully in the parental world by the nature of the expectations of them as workers. The primary obligation of a father to provide economic support coincides nicely with the economic requirement that the majority of men are available for wage labour. It is necessary that other functions attached to the role of the father are vague. Decisions about who cares for a sick child are not made on the basis of an assessment of whom the child needs, but on who should be available because of their role and the routinised status articulations expected of them.[103] These solutions are not child-centred, but are socially determined. Too often it is assumed in social work that it is the needs of children and the emotional make-up of men and women that determine the content of roles, while the requirements of the economic order and their effects on the family are not taken into account.[104] The evidence for this position comes less from descriptions of what is happening in broadly based samples than from the interpretations placed upon selected case material. For example, Dicks, writing on marriage, considers true womanhood is achieved by becoming the wife of a man who is 'somebody' and 'lavishing maternal functions towards *his* children, for *him*'. The male sexual identity is tied to his occupational status and the economic security this brings; both are achieved through his action orientation. Although making the proviso that he is speaking 'in contemporary terms', Dicks proceeds to negate his qualification by designating this allocation of tasks and characteristics as 'biological'.[105] Ackerman takes a similar stance.[106] The implication for practice is that problems can too easily be defined solely in terms of how well or badly parental or marital behaviour fits the traditional role expectations, rather than by using a wider and more complex frame of reference. Kathy Waller,[107] in her survey of the literature on women in families used on social work courses, concluded that, although a number of authors accepted that changes were occurring in the way tasks are allocated in the family, most concentrated on the problems this created rather than looking at the potential it offered. Framed in this way, the treatment emphasis can easily become helping women and men recover their lost identity instead of finding their way through to a new one which is more relevant to the contemporary situation and the demands being made of them.

It is particularly important that social workers are aware of the economic dimensions of role definitions,[108] and the stresses inherent in cultural expectations, because of the temptation to pose the issue in terms of 'through conformity comes sanity'. Talcott Parsons thought otherwise. 'It is quite clear that in the adult feminine role there is quite sufficient strain and insecurity so that widespread manifestations are to be expected in the form of neurotic behaviour.'[109] As a source for male identification he thought the male role also has its problems: the man working away from home leaves an important part of the masculine role unseen so that 'Many masculine functions are of a relatively abstract and intangible character, such that their meaning must be wholly inaccessible to a child.'[110] Talcott Parsons's concern about women's roles has been taken up by a number of sociologists and anthropologists who are in no way advocating an alternative society.[111]

The idea of role presents further problems for social workers, because they frequently practise in situations which, though fulfilling the criterion of being socially recognised, are considered socially undesirable. Some of these relationships are described by the way they default from the prescribed behaviour – the unmarried mother or father, the non-caring parent, the non-custodial parent. Other situations are even more beset by the poverty of language, for instance the non-biological collective or the gay couple lack agreed terms to describe their relationships which are neither derogatory nor reiterate those of the nuclear family. All these relationships are in no way exclusive to the 1970s, they have been with us for centuries, but we do not deign to recognise their validity. A token recognition brings with it dubious advantages. The non-custodial parent seems to have emerged only for the purpose of making him or her invisible. Some of those advocating the exclusion of parents who are no longer undertaking day-to-day care of their children seem to be defining the obligation of the non-custodial parent/s as being to consent to the emptying of their parental role and its complete transfer to other adults.[112] This is in contrast with attempts to develop what Holman has termed 'inclusive' or 'open' foster care,[113] or relationships between parents who, though no longer living together, not only regard continued involvement with the children as a priority, but also extend the circle of concerned persons to the new families of which they have become a part.

It is of little surprise that, applied to the lives of actual people, the idea of role is viewed as oppressive by radical groups. This position is adopted not because they are all existentialists and, following Sartre, consider an active acceptance of role definitions as an evasion of the responsibility to decide, but because the notion of role can be used to deny the validity of experience in order to retain a particular patterning of relationships which is ideologically acceptable. It is oppressive in the liberal sense because it is necessary to redefine social expectations so that they are consistent with existing social and economic conditions; it is oppressive in the left-wing sense because these definitions are necessary for the maintenance of capitalism and patriarchy. In either case they are of dubious value to the practising social worker.

An alternative

It has been suggested that one path to personal liberation is to move from a rigid allocation of behaviour and expectations between the sexes to a recognition of a wide variety of patterns. One suggestion is that we work towards a person who has a balance of those characteristics we have labelled 'masculine' and those we have labelled 'feminine'.[114] There are certain parallels in this with the ideas of writers who contrast hot and cool sex, the open and closed marriage[115] where masculinity and femininity are not clearly defined; 'They are fluid realities, constantly changing and constantly being created.'[116]

Ideal though this may sound as a way through to personhood and liberation from gender stereotypes, McLuhan and Leonard almost lightheartedly point out that this is the way of the world, these are the demands of the new technology. The 'narrow gauge man' with masculine and feminine behaviour kept separate was the ideal of the past. Modern technology requires that he, like Humpty Dumpty, is put together again and, in the short term, some 'feminine' characteristics are being incorporated into masculine behaviour and sensitivity training is considered a valid and laudable activity by business companies. The new technology is complex, responsive, inter-related and the new ideal must reflect this need.[11] All is not liberation, it may become less a rebellion against the straight society than a requirement of its changing shape. The new sexuality certainly takes us away from specialisation, mirroring traditional gender expectations and invalidating behaviour which is neither heterosexual nor genital. There is a move away from the ideal which is clearly patterned — by partner (spouse), by part (genitals), by position (male dominant), by time (night), by place (bedroom)[118] to a wider definition of sexuality which encompasses not only the area of the body and the senses but an exploration of the inner self through religion, drugs or learning through the writings of the mystics to achieve psychic states.[119] McLuhan and Leonard state that researchers who concentrate on how frequently the younger generation participate in genital sex are missing the point. 'How often?' is the concern of the older generation who are obsessed with a definition of sex which equates it with intercourse. The younger generation may well find genital sex less significant than their elders, because it is part of human sexuality and not all of it.[120]

It is clear that sexual activity for men and women outside established pair relationships is becoming more widely accepted because sexual pleasure is valued in itself. Alex Comfort thinks the question is not whether we want this, because it is already happening, but how we learn to handle the complex human problems which result from this particular pattern. It is interesting that on the conscious social level Comfort is acutely aware of the removal of the restraining influence of kin. Although he does not develop his argument in any depth, he seems to see the decrease in the significance of kinship ties as an opportunity to develop a new form of kinship bonds — those of the clan brother or universal kinship by permitting a wider range of sexual relationships.[121]

Comfort appears to be pointing in a similar direction to the women's liberation writers[122] in locating discussions of sexuality within a context. Both sexuality and masculinity-femininity have to be seen within a social structure which is based on patriarchy, in a history of human society where men have used women as exchange objects[123] as a means of breaking into the biological pair in order to cement social relationships.[124] In the economic structure of capitalism other exchange objects (commodities) cement social bonds so that the rule of exogamy and the ban on incest are no longer socially necessary, even though they are retained for ideological reasons.[125]

An analysis which fails to take this into account will produce a struggle for sexual liberation which becomes shadow boxing, not a revolutionary movement. Becoming sexually liberated will be to be liberal, because in the mass society of advanced capitalism sex 'constitutes the last refuge for the myths of individual initiative and sovereignity . . . It promotes sex as the only aspect of life where a certain space still exists for the individual.'[126] The current vogue for sexual paraphernalia, sexual therapy, sexploitation films is not a result of a desire to liberate the oppressed in the political sense. Sociologists and anthropologists are using the terms 'serial marriage' and 'serial polygamy' to describe the present. Group marriage, homosexual marriage, divorce settlements built into marriage contracts, renewable trial marriages, flexible monogamy with 'satellite' relationships all feature in this new free world. They are changes which are recommended in order to make the present social and economic system function more effectively, not to change it. The iron law will fall on those who are the bearers and socialisers of the next generation. There will be all the freedom in the world and none at all.

The nature of the task and its enormity may indeed make some work for the liberation movements look like false starts,[127] but radical movements must attempt to combine action with continuing analysis. In order to re-interpret our conscious and unconscious past the point of departure has to be the oppression experienced at the time. We cannot expect a smooth transition from theory to action, and there will be junctures when action must precede analysis and in some senses supersede what exists. The work of redefinition is arduous, and the order in which we as individuals or collectives proceed will not be logical in the pure, theoretical sense of the word. In a retrospective analysis, actions or issues may be correctly described as misguided, but at the same time they have been an essential stage in the process of becoming politically conscious. If this is true of working in groups outside social work, the problem will be intensified wherever attempts are made to draw the analysis of women's position into social work. We have to make a number of beginnings, recognising that some will be false starts.

6

Towards a conclusion

Historical developments in Great Britain have firmly fixed social work within the framework of state institutions, and teaching and practice has to recognise this fact. The tendency to isolate social work from the context in which it operates has to be resisted because one of the functions of the modern state is to mitigate some of the negative effects of capitalism. Part of this task is allocated to social work and is easily accepted by the members because it coincides with the liberal humanitarian tradition. But limits have to be set to its expression, because while given considerable control over welfare resources and their use, increased social control and rationing powers are also attached. Social workers, like others who find themselves in this position, are faced with the conflicts and contradictions produced by the simultaneous requirement to promote welfare and to protect the economic and social advantages of a class.[1] Reform and welfare provision has to fall short, and demands, even though accepted as reasonable,[2] have to be controlled and sanctions developed. The confusion produced by this power to provide, accompanied by the need and power to ration and control the number of legitimated expectations, is the daily experience of social workers.

Quite apart from their powerlessness to resolve major social problems, there is a tendency to concentrate on relationships because recognition of the causal connections in behaviour is firmly established in social work theory and ideology.[3] However, the theoretical tools available to social workers are much less refined when the objective is to trace the connections between the client's life situations and the socio-economic structure, or for understanding their impact on relationships of race, sex or living in continual poverty.

The offer of an opportunity to demonstrate concern for other human beings and to work towards resolving human problems is, unless severely qualified, to see social workers functioning separately from the economic, social and ideological constraints of the society in which they operate. This creates an unrealistic impression of social worker power that in turn leads to an over-estimation of the degree of change possible for the profession or the individual social worker to achieve.[4] Disillusion becomes inevitable because the extension of the legitimated area of social worker activity is taken to imply an accompanying increase in power to promote change. A major amount of time, however, is diverted from attempts to improve social services, and directed towards trying to prevent the erosion of existing provision and standards.[5] Success can, therefore, often be defined as maintaining what has been achieved rather than moving forward.

An acceptance of this situation and the fact that its origin lies in the function of the state in Britain to protect privilege does not preclude a recognition that the gains achieved can have a significant impact on the lives of people in the here and now.[6] Although the long-term objective is to seek a situation where the profession has become obsolete, this does not mean that the positive part of its present contribution is irrelevant today. The opposition between pressures for present change and relief, and work for a future radical alternative is a luxury possible only for those in a position of privilege who make a theoretical analysis often without a base in experience. The necessity is to keep pressing for change and movement in a way which resists categorisation as 'the solution to the problem'[7] but at the same time to recognise that changes achieved within the existing socio-economic structure will be 'profoundly inadequate'.[8]

A radical seeking an alternative society does not confuse success on one issue with victory, but seeks to acquire the capacity to survive disappointment and continue working and caring. Anger and disgust with what is publicly tolerated is not to be equated with naivety or with the invariable reaction of open conflict. The issues selected for confrontation by the professional are not necessarily those the willing or the unwilling client would choose. An alignment can only be achieved by developing consciousness which is not internal to the profession, however radical social workers may become, but by breaking down barriers between those inside and those outside social work. This cannot be achieved either by social workers standing in a hierarchical relationship to their clients or by attempting to stand apart, but by entering into the 'horizontal interpersonal relationships of men [and women] (my addition) who together unveil the world'.[9] In the British context this means, for a start, establishing links with working-class organisations,[10] liberation movements and collective support groups.

Although analysis of the left-wing radical is made from a Marxist base, this in no way implies that it is irrelevant to master the theories and knowledge held dear by the profession.[11] One of the important tasks of the left-wing radical is to identify points at which the theory and practice of social work is oppressive in terms of class, race and sex. Leonard, for instance, thinks that a primary objective of 'oppositional practice' is to make 'some contribution to transforming a private experience of poverty and exploitation into a manifest expression of class consciousness'.[12] The nature of the contribution will be limited or promoted not only by the agency structure within which the social worker operates but also by the theories and methods available. A knowledge of these is essential in order to make explicit where social work is unhelpful in this process, and, since radical positions are not static, account has to be taken of altered conditions, accumulated experience and what is lost when ideas are absorbed into the liberal tradition.

Sometimes the issue for the left-wing radical student is posed in terms of whether or not to compromise by taking a CQSW course; an alternative approach is to recognise that some compromise is inevitable, that thinking and learning time is a privilege to which there is limited access. The radical has the double task of mastering traditional theory and methods and seeking alternatives. The objective is not to negatively demolish but to accumulate experience which can be fully used to make old structures obsolete after there has been a change in the economic base. This requires the best and not the worst argument or use of skills and these have to be learned. The decision becomes whether the acquisition of knowledge and skills will add to or weaken the long-term collective aim, not whether an individual's conscience is eased by a personal gesture. Left-wing social workers cannot expect comfort, because they are to some extent outsiders in the profession and hence need the support of a group in the wider movement in addition to establishing links with social workers in a similar position. Groups within an agency have to take into account both the power located within it, the external power structures to which it is tied and their interconnected reactions. The desire to make an impact has to be balanced against staying long enough to be able to take effective action.

This action depends on analysis which resists the leap out of historical context by seeing visions of British social workers incorporating directly into their practice elements extracted from

China and Allende's Chile. It is encouraging to read about the socialist objectives of the Schools of Social Work in Chile[13] and learning from their experience is vital, but objectives and action for radical social workers operating under secure capitalism have to take into account the fact that its powers to co-opt and neutralise concepts are as enormous as its powers to control. Attempts to include consciousness-raising into social work activity have to recognise that full social work participation in consciousness-raising activities is possible only when the profession has committed itself to an ideology of liberation.[14] This professional, as opposed to individual, commitment is not possible in Britain because it is not a society going through 'a period of transition towards socialism'.[15] This was the situation described by Alfrero who was careful to locate the objectives of social work in the historical context of Chile during the interlude of a democratically elected Marxist government. In Britain, what is drawn into the profession now has to become liberalised, and the main work undertaken elsewhere.

Just as social work has to be located in the historical context, its value base cannot be discussed without a clear recognition that although socialists and capitalists may join in acclaiming words like 'freedom' and 'justice', detailed formulations will reflect ideological positions between which there is no compromise. These are beginning to be identified in teaching, but more than this is required. Social work values have to be seen not as isolated and protected from contamination by the socio-economic structure within which they operate, but their connection with the predominant economic values and the influence this has on social work practice in the here and now have to be identified. In addition to being an essential stage in working towards the formulation of alternative values for radicals, the task of drawing in this dimension is essential as a preparation for social work practice. It is not a theoretical exercise which can be left to philosophers or sociologists. An examination of the conflicts internal to the professional value system, primarily that between the good of the individual and the good of the community, is a fragile life-line for the newly qualified practitioner because it implies that social work can operate in an unattached way. The process of socialising students into the professional ethos, irrespective of whether or not this base is ideologically acceptable, is insufficient to prepare students for the tasks which they will have to undertake or the conflicts they will inevitably experience.

To imply that, in practice, appeals to humanitarian values are a powerful tool, is to fail to recognise that the wider society, like social work itself, needs checks and balances to maintain its position. These operate upon social work and welfare. Teaching has to avoid presenting social work as a haven from the rat race, a retreat from the effects of competition, or a place where humanitarian values and caring can find fuller expression than elsewhere. The practitioner operates at a meeting-place of the conflicts between the dominant economic values and welfare values as they are defined and accepted within capitalism.

For the left-wing radical, values have an additional dimension; they are not only concerned with attitudes shown during working hours, but with personal values as they affect total living. While self-awareness is part of an attempt to extend the range of relationships within the work setting and can be sought and found within the environs of the profession, conscientisation can only begin when there is an assumption that the social worker stands among, and not apart from, clients. It is alongside them that consciousness-raising activities take place as opposed to within a protected enclave. The use of the term in exercises which begin and end within the profession is questionable. The radical should also attempt to move discussion of values from extolling the virtues of one formulation against the evils of another by seeking to trace and illustrate from experience in Great Britain and internationally the identified and foreseeable practical implications of adopting each position.

Family relationships and their organisation are affected by values and ideology no less than any other area of life. Social work teaching and practice has to locate the family within the economic as well as the cultural context because the family is an economic unit which reflects and perpetuates the socio-economic and patriarchal structure of society. It responds to changes in these structures. This context is vital whether or not the political ideology of the social worker or teacher supports capitalism, since the perspective enables the family to be seen as a dynamic institution subject to complex sources of pressure for change in a technological society. Social workers have to identify the contradictory demands made of it in the requirement to change but to remain the same because the ideology of family has ossified its form. Such knowledge is not just an intellectual pursuit, it is a requirement for practice in work with persons in the family, whether child or adult, because it is here that these pressures and conflicts are experienced. Social workers can contribute by trying to make links between the micro-experience of the family and macro-social issues, in addition to formulating recommendations for social policy changes and service provision.

The predominant patterns of child care are not neutral but differ between societies and in historical periods as studies of both simple and complex cultures demonstrate.[16] Identified children's needs raise questions in teaching about how these are met in a particular society

and why a particular pattern is preferred. A distinction has to
be made between the norm and ideal models because ideals
have to be connected to a particular economic structure
at a point in time, and will present problems for practitioners in a
complex and changing society. Preparation for social work should
include knowledge of the viable range of alternative patterns of child
care so that practitioners can become more receptive to the changes
occuring in their own culture, and be alert to the resource work of
sociologists and anthropologists who trace these changes and explore
their positives and negatives. To make a contribution to clients
experiencing the effects of these dynamics in their lives a movement
from the position of regarding social work as Canute-like, protecting
clients from the impact of technological change, has to take place.
Connections between the social and cultural past and present should
be drawn into relationship work in addition to the psychological
dimension.

These issues are directly related to whether or not the profession
wishes to support the nuclear stable family as an ideal — or whether
to move towards making explicit a recognition of a range of viable
alternative models, including the collective situation. If the latter
position is adopted the debate then moves to exploring what issues
and tasks are raised for social work by acknowledging that a range
of patterns are possible within a complex culture. One task towards
which social work could contribute is to identify the problems
thought to pertain to each model, to try to locate their source or
sources, and to consider whether and what ways through can be found.

The current tendency to equate meeting children's needs and
nuclear family life produces a concentration on how people in
parenting situations differ from each other — the one parent is
contrasted with the two, the two with the collective, the gay with the
heterosexual. Because they are seen as different, the needs they have in
common[17] are under-estimated. Alongside common human needs, and
children's needs, teaching is required on the generic needs of
parenthood. Factors which, at present, are seen as specific and internal
to a model may more correctly be viewed as a matter of degree than of
absolute difference. For instance, is the emotional pressure on
one-parent families different in degree or kind from that on two-parent
families where the time and energies of one are engaged in work
pursuits for a significant proportion of their time — for example the
seaman, the long-distance lorry driver, the executive, the
psychotherapist — or do both suffer from a poverty of relationships
which result in part from work patterns, from urban living and
geographical mobility? Similar questions arise in relation to parenting
in poverty, irrespective of the numbers of parenting figures involved.

95

If the emphasis moves in this direction, other areas for development emerge. It is generally agreed that children need stable relationships, but can this be equated with nuclear family stability or are there other alternative ways of providing it, and how can they be developed? The way issues are formulated in theory has a profound effect on what is thought possible for practice. If there is a simple equation between nuclear family stability and a good enough experience for the child, practice intervention has, at all costs, to be directed towards creating nuclear families where none exists and maintaining them where they do. If not, a whole range of possibilities arise.[18] The degree to which social work can contribute to this process is linked to the reason certain economic and social negatives attracted to particular models are tolerated socially or even thought desirable. Thus, identified and continuing public — as opposed to private — neglect has to be distinguished from anomalies that are no longer relevant to retain. In the first instance, the public neglect is accepted because to remove or alleviate it would have a major impact on the social structure and here social work can have little effect without there being prior movements in the general society. The position is not, however, static and areas where there is room for movement exist alongside others where, at present, little or none is possible.

A recognition of, or a commitment to, a range of models within which caring can take place means that developmental tasks have to be examined as they affect the range of models, and because a substantial minority of children and adults move between them the tasks involved in this process have to be identified and ways of accomplishing them explored. This is an area requiring an enormous amount of work, since although social work intervention tends to be an interlude, it can occur at any point along the dynamic. Adding isolated interventions into a continuous narrative produces a heavy weighting of negatives, distorting experience and limiting perceived potential. To the in-depth study in the short term, the long-term detailed study has to be added as a resource for practitioners so their intervention can be related to a whole. The radical of whatever persuasion can take an active part in ensuring that academic longitudinal studies are linked with the analysis of groups who are structuring their own experience, and that practice is influenced.

A precondition of participation in this process of becoming open about a range of family situations is that the social worker has faced and made some steps in taking hold of his or her own family experience. Self-awareness cannot be confined to the exceptional — the baby batterer, the commune, the gay parent — each person's experience of the norm is involved as well as their departures from it. Failing this, it is impossible to tolerate diversity without equating it with chaos, or to recognise that chaos can and does exist in the experience of some people, irrespective of the family model in which they live.

The family is central in definition of femininity, it is the place where, through their men and children, women are traditionally thought to find their fulfilment psychologically. They take their social position from it whereas men's originates from their activities outside. Sufficient theoretical work has been carried out, that only in part originates from women's and gay liberation, to merit a major re-examination of the theories about masculinity, femininity and sexuality offered to social workers as a basis for their practice. At the minimum, the debates need drawing into teaching and where possible their implications for practice identified. This involves a thorough re-examination of the literatures used in human growth and development sequences and elsewhere in the curriculum to ensure that alternative views and resource material is at least shown to exist. A major impetus must come from students, teachers and practitioners who are involved in the women's and gay liberation movements, but even within the traditional approach it is not at all clear that the past cultural preferences for a particular type of masculinity and femininity and pattern of sexual responses will be those of the future. The introduction or re-introduction of cross-cultural studies could, if used in a way which connects our own pattern to the range existing in human societies, sensitise students and workers to the variations and changes occuring within their own, some of which have been validated by statute.

It is necessary in teaching about our own society to move from repetitive studies on the effects of a working mother on her children to looking in greater depth at some of the issues raised for men and women being, or children having, working parents, the positives and negatives which result from this, as well as the type of social or community resources necessary to supplement parental care. Similarly, to a study of life in the differentiated family, has to be added that of the family in which functions are allocated from preference or for convenience on a non-sex-typed basis. Further questions have to be asked about the implications of changes in the way caring and nurturing functions are allocated inside and outside the family on a non-sex basis to people who, however committed, carry to a greater or lesser extent within themselves the traditional, cultural expectations. Participation in analysing this process of change is not, as some claim, the prerogative of the bourgeoisie, it is an essential task of each generation and class; nor is the work something new which evolved from a knowledge of psychoanalytic method. The fact that bourgeois analysis and ideology predominates should not be confused with the absence of analysis by the working class or with a lack of capacity for it.[19] To respond to and promote further opportunities for its development, social work needs, as a resource, a background which allows alternative resolutions.

Human growth and development sequences have often failed to move, or have moved only marginally, to take into account societal shifts which have been marked by legislation. The issue has been raised of whether teaching on homosexuality can appropriately be dealt with in sequences on psychiatry,[20] or whether sexuality can fully be accounted for by teaching about the psychosexual development of young children or family planning techniques. A reassessment of the content of these sequences would help social workers to face the issues being raised by homosexual parenting or men and women testing the boundaries of conventional sexual behaviour; it would also help them to respond to men, women and adolescents who are trying to work out these questions within a fairly conventional framework.

The degree of movement taking place and the range of patterns emerging brings into doubt the application of basic role definitions. Expectations and obligations attached to these roles originate from analysis of what is past and have to assume consensus. The contemporary situation and the conflicts within it cannot be taken fully into account. The legislative changes in the areas of race, sex and sexual preference have provided an impetus, the effects of which have not yet been fully identified, understood or lived through. There are men who wish to foster but, unlike single women, are excluded by the regulations,[21] while at the same time men on their own have been given the same rights as women to decide whether or not they wish to stay at home to look after their children or go to work. The cohabitation rule becomes more difficult to administer when there is even a beginning acceptance that women can seek economic and sexual independence, instead of dependence and exclusive sex within marriage. Basic role definitions remain useful as reference points for both our social and psychological historical past, but their limitations in practice have to be clearly identified. Situational analysis, by offering a structure to look at how decisions are made, the differing patterns of priorities, is a more useful tool for practitioners whose concern is to identify what stresses exist for clients, their source and possible ways of resolving them.

Finally, although the left-wing social worker needs to retain and develop links with movements in the wider society, because it is from these that the major impetus towards radical alternatives comes, it is possible to utilise to some extent this experience within social work. Restraints exist in all contemporary work situations, but what seems impossible at one period becomes possible in another, the radicals of one generation are turned into liberals by the next.

NOTES

Chapter 1 Radicalism and social work

1   Lees, R., 'Politics and Social Work', Routledge & Kegan Paul, London, 1972.
2   E.g. BASW, 'Social Action and Social Work. Report of the Working Party on Social Action', BASW Publication 6, 1974; and Bailey, R. and Brake, M. (eds), 'Radical Social Work', Edward Arnold, London, 1975.
3   BASW, op. cit.
4   Cypher, J., Social Reform and the Social Work Profession, in Jones, H. (ed.), 'Towards a New Social Work', Routledge & Kegan Paul, London, 1975, p.17.
5   Rose, H. and Hamner, J., Community Participation and Social Change, in Jones, D. and Mayo, M. (eds), 'Community Work Two', Routledge & Kegan Paul, London, 1975, pp.25-45.
6   Sherwell, 1898, quoted in Seed, P., 'The Expansion of Social Work in Britain', Routledge & Kegan Paul, London, 1973, p.36.
7   Mitchell, J., 'Psychoanalysis and Feminism', Penguin, Harmondsworth, 1975, and for an opposite point of view, Brooks, K., Freudianism is Not a Basis for a Marxist Psychology, in Brown, P. (ed.), 'Radical Psychology', Tavistock Publications, London, 1973, pp.315-74.
8   Mitchell, J., op. cit. and Cooper, D., 'Grammar of Living', Allen Lane, London, 1974.
9   Roszak, T., 'The Making of a Counter Culture', Faber & Faber, London, 1970.
10 Laing, R.D., 'The Politics of Experience and the Bird of Paradise', Penguin, Harmondsworth, 1967, p.119.
11 Roszak, T., op.cit.
12 Bourstein, D., The Power to Leap, The Reith Lectures, 'Listener', BBC Publications, London, 3 December 1975.
13 In Illich, I., 'Celebrations of Awareness', Penguin, Harmondsworth, 1973, pp.9-10.
14 Ibid., p.119.

99

15   Resnick, R.P., Conscientisation: An Indigenous Approach to International Social Work, 'International Social Work', Vol.XIX, no.1, 1976.
16   DHSS classification in 'Health and Personal Social Services Statistics', HMSO, London, 1974.
17   Bender, F., and Clark, E.I., Does Faculty Congruence Work?The Case of Social Work Education, 'Canadian Journal of Social Work Education', vol.I, no.1, autumn 1973, p.13.
18   Epstein, I., The Politics of Behaviour Therapy in the New Cool-out Casework, in Jones, H. (ed.), op.cit., p.139.
19   Specht, H., The Deprofessionalism of Social Work, 'Social Work', NASW, March 1972, pp.3-5.
20   Pearson, G., The Politics of Uncertainty: A Study in the Socialisation of Social Workers, in Jones, H. (ed.), op.cit., pp.50-60.
21   Goldstein, H., 'Social Work: A Unitary Approach', University of South Carolina Press, Columbia, 1973, ch.3.
22   Employers and Workmen's Act 1875, Home Secretary speaking on, quoted in Lewis, N., Statute, The Merchant Shipping Act 1970, 'Modern Law Review', vol.34, January 1975, p.55.
23   For a discussion see Maluccio, A.N. and Marlow, W.D., The Case for the Contract, 'Social Work', NASW, vol.19, no.1, January 1974, pp.35-8; and CCETSW, 'Values in Social Work', Paper 13, CCETSW, 1976, pp.31-3.
24   'Claimants Union Newspaper.'
25   Bitensky, R., Influence of Political Power in Social Work, 'Journal of Social Policy', vol.2, part 2, April 1973, p.127.
26   Cooper, D., op.cit. pp.15-16, and Leonard, P., Towards a Paradigm for Radical Practice in Social Work, in Bailey, R. and Brake, M., op.cit., pp.46-61.
27   Marshall, T.H., 'Social Policy', Hutchinson, London, 1970, pp.96-7.
28   Leonard, P., op.cit., p.49.
29   Private communication with a current researcher. The variables she has identified include, in addition to those mentioned, state registration or endorsement for social workers (France, Belgium, Czechoslovakia, South Africa, Argentina, Brazil, Germany); a national curriculum (France, Norway, Sweden, Austria, Czechoslovakia, Brazil, Sri Lanka); state examinations (Belgium, France); state initiated reform of social work education (New Zealand, Argentina, Norway, Sweden); state run social work education (Sri Lanka, Cyprus, Turkey). On the other hand, America, Canada, Switzerland and the Netherlands have a high degree of professional control over social work education. See also Kendall K. Cross, 'National Review of Social Work Education', paper given at the XVII International Congress of Schools of Social Work, Nairobi, 6-9 June 1974, on signifi-cance of state finance in the development of social work education.
30   Stein, H., Reflections on Practice Policy, quoted in Resnick, R.P., Conscientisation: an Indigenous Approach to International Social Work', 'International Social Work', vol.XIX, no.1, 1976.
31   Wilson, L., 'Women and the Welfare State', 'Red Rag', Pamphlet no.2, 9 Stratford Villas, London NW1. No date.
32   Hunter, D.R., Social Action to Influence Institutional Change, 'Social Casework', FSA, America, April 1970, p.230.
33   BASW (1974) op.cit., para. 6.1.
34   Private communication with Brian Cohen, Community Work Course, Goldsmiths College, London.
35   BASW, 'The Inalienable Element in Social Work', BASW Publications and 'Social Work Today', vol.4, no.1, 5 April 1973.

36   Edward Norman, Lecturer in Modern History, Peterhouse, Cambridge
      reached a similar conclusion about The Church in Class, Culture and
      Clerisy, BBC Radio 3, 24 November 1975.
37   Quoted by Cypher, J., in Jones, H. (ed.), op.cit., p.9.
38   BASW (1974), op.cit., para.6.1.
39   BASW's lobby against the fostering clauses in the 1975 Children's Act
      illustrates both these points. It failed to achieve any major changes in the
      bill.
40   Bitensky, R., op.cit., p.140.
41   See Durkin, L. and Douieb, B., The Mental Patients' Union, in Jones, D.
      and Mayo, M. (eds), op.cit., pp.177-91, and the 'Claimants' Union
      Newspaper'.
42   Ginsberg, M.I., Changing Values in Social Work, in Kendall, K. (ed.),
      'Social Work Values in an Age of Discontent', Council of Social Work
      Education, New York, 1970, pp.22-4.
43   Report of the Committee on Local Authority and Allied Personal Social
      Services (Seebohm Report), HMSO, London Cmnd. 3703, 1968, para.628.
44   George, V. and Wilding, P. 'Motherless Families', Routledge & Kegan Paul,
      London, 1972, p.154.
45   Mitchell, J., 'Women's Estate', Penguin, Harmondsworth, 1971, pp.84-6,
      et seq.
46   Epstein, I., Professionalisation, Professionalism and Social Worker
      Radicalism, 'Journal of Health and Social Behaviour', March 1969,
      pp.67-77.
47   Specht, H., op.cit.
48   Alinsky, S., 'Rules for Radicals', Vintage Books, New York, 1972.
49   Marcuse, H., Varieties of Humanism, 'Center Magazine', Center for the
      Study of Democratic Institutions, Santa Barbara, June 1968. Quoted in
      Roszak, op.cit., p.71, and see Neville, R., 'Play Power', Paladin, London,
      1971, pp.55-6.
50   BASW (1974) op.cit., para. 2.2.1.
51   Jackson, G. 'Soledad Brother: The Prison Letters of George Jackson',
      Penguin, Harmondsworth, 1971.
52   Crowther, G., Self-sufficiency, Rural Commune – Special Offer,
      'Bitbetter', London, no.13, 1975, pp.13-16.
53   'Case Con', spring 1975, p.2.
54   Jackson, G., op.cit., p.71.
55   'Case Con', op.cit., p.2.
56   Friere, P., 'Pedagogy of the Oppressed', Penguin, Harmondsworth,
      London, 1972, p.60.
57   Steiner, C., Radical Psychiatry and Movement Groups in 'The Radical
      Therapist', Radical Therapist Collective, Penguin, Harmondsworth,
      London, 1974, p.39.
58   Friere, P., op.cit.
59   Cooper, D. (1974), op.cit., p.148.
60   Cooper, D., 'Death of the Family', Allen Lane, London, 1971, pp.46-7
      and 75-82.
61   Friere, P., op.cit. and Illich, I., op.cit.
62   Resnick, R.P., op.cit., p.24.
63   Mitchell, J. (1971), op.cit., p.63, and see Alfrero, L.A., Conscientisation,
      in 'New Themes in Social Work Education', International Schools of
      Social Work, 1972. Proceedings of XVI International Congress of
      Schools of Social Work.

64   Stein, H., op.cit., p.27.
65   Flack, R., and Grayer, E.D., A Consciousness-raising Group for Obese Women, 'Social Work', NASW, November 1975, pp.484-7.
66   Friere, P., op.cit., pp.22 and 25.
67   Connerton, P., The Collective Historical Subject. Reflections on Lukacs' 'History and Class Consciousness', 'British Journal of Sociology', vol.XXV, no.2, June 1974, p.171. Jung comes close to expressing a similar idea: 'In psychology one possesses nothing unless one has experienced it in reality. Hence a purely intellectual insight is not enough because one knows only the words and not the substance of the thing from the inside.' 'Aion', Routledge & Kegan Paul edn., London, 1959, p.33.
68   Kendall, K., Eileen Younghusband Lecture, given at the National Institute for Social Work, London, October 1972.
69   Illich, I., op.cit., p.22.
70   Lerner, B., 'Therapy in the Ghetto: Political Impotence and Personal Disintegration', Johns Hopkins University Press, Baltimore, 1972, p.62, quoted in Preface to Goodman, J.A. (ed.), 'The Dynamics of Racism in Social Work Practice', NASW, Washington, 1973, p.xiii.
71   Friere, P., op.cit.
72   For an attempt, see Sim, S., Conversations with Archie, 'Case Con', no.19.
73   Social Work in Search of a Radical Profession, in Rein, M., 'Social Policy', Random House, New York, 1970, ch.15.
74   Cooper, D. (ed.), 'Dialectics of Liberation', Penguin, Harmondsworth, 1968, pp.9-10.
75   See Mitchell, J. op.cit., p.207.
76   See works of Friere, Laing, Cooper.
77   Friere, P., op.cit., p.42.
78   Roszak, T., op.cit., ch.4.
79   'Case Con', no.18, January 1975, p.2.
80   Lide, P., Dialogue on Racism. A prologue for Action, in Goodman, J.A., (ed.), op.cit., pp.12-21.
81   Friere, P., op.cit., p.42.
82   Keith Lucas, A., Alliances for Power, 'Social Work', NASW, vol.20, no.2, March 1975, pp.93-7.

Chapter 2   Values and social work

1   Youth in the Context of American Society, in Erikson, E. (ed.), 'Youth Change and Challenge', Basic Books, New York, 1963, pp.98-102.
2   See Downie, R.S., 'Roles and Values', Methuen, London, 1971, pp.78-9 for a discussion.
3   George, V. and Wilding, P., Social Values and Social Policy, 'Journal of Social Policy', vol.4, no.4, pp.373-90.
4   Tawney, R.H., 'Religion and the Rise of Capitalism', Penguin, Harmondsworth, 1961.
5   Ibid., p.247, and see also Benn, S.I. and Peters, R.S., 'The Democratic State', Allen & Unwin, London, 1959, pp.24-8.
6   Marcuse, H., 'Eros and Civilisation', Abacus edn., Sphere Books, London, 1972, p.12, and 'One Dimensional Man', Abacus edn., Sphere Books, London, 1972.
7   Mitchell, J., 'Women's Estate', Penguin, Harmondsworth, 1971, p.176.

8 Marcuse, H., 'Eros and Civilisation', op.cit., p.12.

9 Marcuse, H., 'One Dimensional Man', op.cit., p.195.

10 Marcuse, H., 'Eros and Civilisation', op.cit., p.12.

11 Ibid., p.12.

12 Cooper, D., 'Grammar of Living', Allen Lane, London, 1974, p.148.

13 Report of the Committee on Local Authority and Allied Personal Social Services (Seebohm Report), HMSO, London, Cmnd. 3703, 1968, paras. 427-30.

14 Downie, R.S., op.cit., p.2.

15 Marx, K., in Bottomore, T.B. and Rubel, M., 'Selected Writings in Sociology and Social Philosophy', Penguin, Harmondsworth, 1961, p.87.

16 E.g. 'Values in Social Work', CCETSW, Paper 13, 1976, pp.36-7. In the case illustration given the appeal to values gives no guide to what action can be taken. The decision is based on practical issues such as the need to maintain relationships with other agency workers, and the 'role and function' of the social worker.

17 Marx, K., in Bottomore, T.B. and Rubel, M., op.cit., p.93.

18 Biesteck, L., Basic Values in Social Work and Problems in Identifying Social Work Values, in NASW Regional Institute Programme, Monograph IX, 'Values in Social Work Re-examined', New York, 1972, p.20.

19 Holman, R., Poverty: Consensus and Alternatives, 'British Journal of Social Work', vol.3, no.4, winter 1973, pp.431-46, and Ryan, W., 'Blaming the Victim', Vintage Books, New York, 1972.

20 Cooper, D., 'Death of the Family', Allen Lane, London, 1974.

21 Freud, A., Children Possessed, 'Child Adoption', no.3, 1975, p.40.

22 Alinsky, S., 'Rules for Radicals', Vintage Books, New York, 1972, pp.44-5.

23 Mishra, R., Marx and Welfare, 'Sociological Review', vol.23, no.2, new series, pp.287-313.

24 Parkin, F., 'Class Inequality and the Political Order', Paladin, London, 1971.

25 'Values in Social Work', CCETSW, op.cit., p.29.

26 Fetscher, I., Marx's Concretization of the Concept of Freedom, in McDermott, F.E. (ed.), 'Self-determination in Social Work', Routledge & Kegan Paul, 1975, p.181.

27 Bird, C., 'The Invisible Scar', McKay, New York, 1966, quoted in Howard, D., 'Social Welfare: Values, Means and Ends, Random House, New York, 1969, p.321.

28 For a discussion see Howard, D., op.cit.

29 Ryan, W., op.cit.

30 For a full discussion see Fetscher, I. Marx's Concretization of the Concept of Freedom in McDermott, F.E. (ed.), op.cit., pp.181-91.

31 Young, J., 'The Drug Takers', Paladin, London, 1971, and Brown, P. (ed.), 'Radical Psychology', Tavistock, London, 1973, for a collection of perspectives on this point.

32 Anti-mass: Collectives as a Form of Organisation, 'Bitbetter', no.13, London, 1975, pp.20-7.

33 George, V. and Wilding, P., op.cit.

34 Perlman, S., Self Determination: Reality or Illusion (1965) reprinted in McDermott, F.E., op.cit., pp.66-7.

35 Parsons, Talcott, Youth in the Context of American Society in 'Youth, Change and Challenge', E.M. Erikson, (ed.), Basic Books, New York, 1963, p.96.

36 Biesteck, L., op.cit.

37   Perlman, S., op.cit.
38   Ibid., pp.74-5.
39   Bernstein, S., Conflict, Self-determination and Social Work, in NASW
     Monograph IX, 'Values in Social Work Reexamined', NASW Regional
     Institute Program, NASW, New York, 1967.
40   Keith Lucas, A., Self-determination and the Changing Role of the
     Worker, in NASW Monograph, op.cit., p.90.
41   Friere, P., 'Pedagogy of the Oppressed', Penguin, Harmondsworth,
     London, 1972, and Alfrero, L.A., Conscientisation, in 'New Themes in
     Social Work Education', International Schools of Social Work, 1972.
     Proceedings of the XVI International Congress of Schools of Social Work.
42   Parsons, T., op.cit., pp.96 and 98.
43   I am indebted to a colleague, Elizabeth Wulff-Cochrane, for this point.
44   See Pearson, G., The Making of Social Workers, in Brake, M. and Bailey,
     R. (eds), 'Radical Social Work', Edward Arnold, London, 1975, ch.2.
45   Wilding, P. and George, V., 'Motherless Families', Routledge & Kegan
     Paul, London, 1972.
46   Pumphrey, M., 'The Teaching of Values and Ethics in Social Work
     Education', CSWE, New York, 1959, p.61.
47   Lees, R., 'Politics and Social Work', Routledge & Kegan Paul, London, 1972.
48   Ginsberg, M.I., Changing Values in Social Work in Kendall, K., (ed.),
     'Social Work Values in an Age of Discontent', Council on Social Work
     Education, New York, 1970, p.28.
49   Keith Lucas, A., 'Decision about People in Need', University of North
     Carolina Press, Chapel Hill, 1957.
50   DHSS, 'The Supplementary Benefits Handbook' was first published in
     1970 and is periodically revised. See also Stevenson, O., 'Claimant or
     Client', Allen & Unwin, London, 1973.
51   Stevenson, O., op.cit.
52   For an example, see Laing, W.A., 'Cost Benefits of Family Planning', PEP,
     London 1972.
53   Tropp, E., Three Problematic Concepts: Client, Helper, Worker, in
     'Social Casework', January 1974, vol.55, no.1, pp.21-2.
54   Ibid.
55   Carmichael, K., The Relation of Social Work Departments and the DHSS,
     in Newman, N. (ed.), 'In Cash or Kind: The Place of Financial Assistance
     in Social Work', Department of Social Administration, University of
     Edinburgh, November 1974, p.64.
56   Hepworth, D.H. and Shumway, E.G., Changes in Open-mindedness as a
     Result of Social Work Education, 'Journal for Social Work', vol.12, no.1,
     winter 1976, pp.56-62.
57   McCulloch, J.W. and Smith, N.J., Blacks and Social Work, 'New Society',
     25 April 1974, pp.191-2.
58   Varley, B., Social Work Values, 'Journal of Education for Social Work',
     vol.4, no.2, autumn 1968, pp.67-76.
59   Witte, E.F., Student Wisdom and Values: The Positive Force of
     Disaffection, in Kendall, K. (ed.), op.cit.
60   Wilson, D., Uneasy Bedfellows, 'Social Work Today', vol.5, no.1, April
     1975, p.12.
61   Marx, K., in Bottomore, T.B. and Rubel, M., op.cit., p.92.
62   BASW, The Inalienable Element in Social Work, BASW Publications and
     'Social Work Today', vol.4, no.1, 5 April 1973, p.17, para. 5.
63   Lenin, V., 'What Is to Be Done?', Foreign Languages Publishing House,
     Moscow, 1974 edn., p.39.

Chapter 3 The family

1	Quoted by Kellmer Pringle, M., in 'Concern', no.17, National Children's Bureau, summer 1975, p.6.
2	Cooper, J., in 'The Family in Society, Dimensions of Parenthood', HMSO, London, 1974.
3	Coser, R.L. (ed.), 'The Family, its Functions and Structure', 1st ed., St Martins Press, New York, 1964, p.xxvii.
4	Bronfenbrenner, U., 'Two Worlds of Childhood, US and USSR', Russell Sage Foundation, New York, and Allen & Unwin, London, 1971; and Kessen, W. (ed.), 'Childhood in China', Yale University Press, New Haven, 1975.
5	Keller, S., Does the Family have a Future? in Coser, R.L. (ed.), 'The Family, its Functions and Structure', 2nd ed., Macmillan, London, 1974, pp.579-82.
6	Coser, R.L. (ed.), op.cit., 1st ed., 1964, p.xxvii.
7	Sharpe, S., 'The Role of the Nuclear Family in the Oppression of Women in The Body Politic: Women's Liberation in Great Britain', Stage 1, Theobalds Rd, London WC1, 1972, p.145.
8	Davis, K., in Coser, R.L. (ed.), op.cit., p.448.
9	Mitchell, J., 'Psychoanalysis and Feminism', Penguin, Harmondsworth, 1975, p.411.
10	Horkheimer, M., (ed.), 'Sozialpsychologischer Teil in Autoritaet und Familie', Librairie Alcan, Paris, 1936, p.87, quoted in Coser, R.L. (ed), op.cit., 2nd ed., p.xvi.
11	Malinowski, B., The Principle of Legitimacy, in Coser, R.L. (ed.), (1974), op.cit., 2nd ed., pp.58-63.
12	Report of the Committee on One-parent Families (Finer Report), HMSO, London, Cmnd. 5629-1, 1975, vol.2, Appendix, Finer, M. and McGregor, O.M., The History of the Obligation to Maintain, p.95.
13	Lévi-Strauss, C., 'Structural Anthropology', Allen Lane, London, 1968. For a discussion see Mitchell, J. (1975), op.cit., pp.371-6.
14	Heraud, B., 'Sociology for Social Workers', Pergamon Press, Oxford, 1970, p.65.
15	Davids, L., 'New Family Forms', in Francoeur, R. and A. (eds), 'The Future of Sexual Relations', Spectrum, New Jersey, 1974, and Mead, M., Marriage in Two Steps, in Otto, H.A. (ed.), 'The Family in Search of a Future', Appleton Century Crofts, New York, 1970, pp.75-85.
16	Comfort, A., Sexuality in a Zero Growth Culture, in Francoeur, R. and A. (eds), op.cit., pp.52-7.
17	Parkin, F., 'Class, Inequality and the Political Order', Paladin, London, 1972, pp.66-8.
18	Weber, M., quoted in Parkin, F., ibid., p.161.
19	Mitchell, J., 'Women's Estate', Penguin, Harmondsworth, 1971, p.155.
20	Parsons, T., The Incest Taboo in Relation to the Social Structure, in Coser, R.L. (ed), op.cit., 1st edn, 1964, p.50; see also Lévi-Strauss, op.cit.
21	Raynor, E., 'Human Development', Allen & Unwin, London, 1971, p.51.
22	Engels, F., 'Origin of the Family and Private Property', 1891, in Marx, K., and Engels, F., 'Selected Works' in one volume, Lawrence & Wishart, London, 1970, p.451.
23	Parsons, T., op.cit., p.50.
24	Mitchell, J. (1975), op.cit., p.370.
25	Ibid. For a discussion see pp.370-6.

26   Ibid., p.408.
27   Seglow, J., Pringle, K.P., Wedge, P., 'Growing Up Adopted', NFER, 1972, pp.96-7. Seven per cent of adopted children were not living with both their adoptive parents by the age of seven. George, V., 'Foster Care', Routledge & Kegan Paul, London, 1970, pp.115-19.
28   Laslett, P., 'The World We Have Lost', Methuen, London, 1965.
29   Oakley, A., 'Housewife', Allen Lane, London, 1974.
30   Finer, M. and McGregor, O.R., Appendix to Finer Report, op.cit.
31   E.g. 'The Shorter English Dictionary', Oxford University Press, London, 1973.
32   Cuber, J.F., Alternative Models from the Perspective of Sociology, in Otto, H.A. (ed.), op.cit., p.11.
33   Morton, P., A Woman's Work is Never Done, 'Leviathan', vol. II, no.1, p.34, quoted in Mitchell, J. (1971), op.cit., p.152.
34   Cuber, J.F., op.cit., p.13.
35   Alexander, S., The Night Cleaners: An Assessment of the Campaign, 'Red Rag', Pamphlet no.6, 9 Stratford Villas, London NW1. No date.
36   Laing, R.D. and Esterson, A., 'Sanity, Madness and the Family', Tavistock Publications, London, 1964.
37   Berlin, I., 'Two Concepts of Liberty: An Inaugural Lecture', Oxford University Press, London, 1958.
38   See also Holman, R., Are Second Thoughts Best on the Children's Bill?, 'Community Care', vol.1, no.1, 1975.
39   Pringle, M.K., Setting the Scene, 'Concern', no.17, summer 1975, p.8.
40   Wall, W.D., Constructive Education, 'Concern', no.17, summer 1975, p.13.
41   Mead, M., op.cit.
42   Davids, L., op.cit.
43   Erikson, E., op.cit.
44   Holman, R., op.cit., and BASW Annual Report, 1974-5, p.21, para. 13.2.
45   Lesbians, Marriage and Motherhood, in Gay Issue of 'Case Con', no.18, January 1975.
46   E.g. Seglow, J., Pringle, K.P. and Wedge, P., op.cit.; Crellin, E., Pringle, K.P., and West, P., 'Born Illegitimate', NFER, 1971; Davie, R., Butler, N. and Goldstein, H., 'From Birth to Seven: A Report of the National Child Development Study', Longman Group, London, in association with the National Children's Bureau, 1972.
47   Wilson, H. and Herbert, G.W., Parenting in Poverty, 'British Journal of Social Work', vol.4, no.3, autumn 1974, pp.241-54, and Wilson, H., Delinquency in the Inner City, 'Social Work Today', vol.5, no.15, 31 October 1974, pp.446-9.
48   Douglas, J.W.B., 'The Home and the School', MacGibbon & Kee, London, 1964.
49   Stevenson, O., Rapporteurs Observations, in 'The Family in Society, Dimensions of Parenthood', op.cit., p.106.
50   The Children Act 1975.
51   BASW 5th Annual Report, July 1974 - March 1975, Section 3 Child Care and the Family, para. 13.2, p.21.
52   Parsons, T., op.cit., p.52.
53   See Otto, H.A. (ed.), op.cit., and Francoeur, R. and A. (eds), op.cit., for the use of these terms.
54   Goldberg, E.M., The Normal Family — A Myth or Reality, in Younghusband, E., 'Social Work With Families', Allen & Unwin, London, 1965.

55 Ferri, E., 'Growing Up in a One-parent Family', in 'Concern', National Children's Bureau, no.20, summer 1976; and Ferri, E. and Robinson, H., 'Coping Alone', National Children's Bureau, 1975. For an American study see Sauber, M. and Corrigan, E.M., 'The Six-year Experience of Unwed Mothers', Research Department, Community Council of Greater New York, New York, 1970.

56 Report of the Care of Children Committee (Curtis Report), HMSO, London, Cmnd 6922, 1946.

57 Kellmer Pringle, M., Letter to 'New Society', July 1972.

58 Joseph, Sir K., Speech to the Annual Conference of the National Children's Bureau, Sheffield, 22 September 1972, p.20 of copy of speech.

59 Seglow, J., Pringle, K.P. and Wedge, P., op.cit.

60 Ibid., p.161.

61 Ferri, E., op.cit., p.9.

62 Pringle, M. K., Letter to 'New Society', July 1972.

63 Finer Report, vol.I, op.cit., para. 9.3, p.490.

64 Bronfenbrenner, U., Children, Families and Social Policies: An American Perspective, in 'The Family in Society, Dimensions of Parenthood', HMSO, 1974.

65 Ferri, E., op.cit., p.9.

66 Lipman-Blumen, J., The Implications for Family Structure of Changing Sex-roles, 'Social Casework', February 1976, pp.67-79.

67 Finer Report, op.cit., vol.I, para. 3.59, pp.58-9.

68 Laing, W.A., 'Cost and Benefits of Family Planning', PEP, London, 1972.

69 Bronfenbrenner, U., (1971), op.cit., pp.140-1.

Chapter 4 The Family: alternatives

1 Cooper, D., 'Grammar of Living', Allen Lane, London, 1974, and·Reich, R., 'Sexuality and Class Struggle', Praeger Publishers, New York, 1971.

2 Reich, R., ibid., Ch.7.

3 Alfrero, L.A., Conscientisation, in 'New Themes in Social Work Education', International Schools of Social Work, 1972. Proceedings of XVI International Congress of Schools of Social Work, p.77.

4 Ibid., p.76.

5 Brake, M., Lecturer, Kent University, comments on draft of this chapter.

6 Reich, R., op.cit.

7 Cooper, D., 'Death of the Family', Allen Lane, London, 1971, pp.46-7.

8 For heterosexual couple life without children, see Peck, E., 'The Baby Trap', Heinrich Hanau Publications, London, 1973, and Humphrey, M., 'The Hostage Seekers', Longmans, London, 1969. For homosexual relationships, see Wittman, C., Gay Liberation Manifesto, in 'The Radical Therapist', Radical Therapist Collective, Penguin, Harmondsworth, 1974, pp.171-483.

9 There is a growing amount of literature on the potential for mental health in later life, see Rutter, M., 'Maternal Deprivation, Reassessed', Penguin, Harmondsworth, 1972, and Morgan, P., 'Child Care Sense and Fable', Maurice Temple Smith, London, 1975, and Kadushin, A., 'Adopting Older Children', Columbia University Press, New York, 1970.

10 Cooper, D., 'Death of the Family', op.cit., pp.9-15.

11 Brake, M., comments on draft of this chapter.

12 Some literature is emerging, for instance, Richman, J., Goldthorp, W.O.

and Simmons, C., Fathers in Labour, 'New Society', 13 October 1975, or Brown, J.L., The Role of Grandparents in Carrying the Moral, Ethical and Cultural Values to the New Generation, in 'Family Involvement', Browndale, Canada, September 1975.

13   Bronfenbrenner, U., 'Two Worlds of Childhood USA and USSR', Russell Sage Foundation, New York and Allen and Unwin, London, 1971, p.95.

14   Goldstein, J., Freud, A., Solneit, A.J., 'Beyond the Best Interests of the Child', Collier Macmillan, London, 1973, p.20.

15   Bronfenbrenner, U., op.cit., p.95.

16   Mitchell, J., 'Psychoanalysis and Feminism', Penguin, Harmondsworth, 1975, p.378.

17   Winnicott, D.W., Contemporary Concepts of Adolescent Development, in Winnicott, D.W., 'Playing and Reality', Tavistock Publications, London, 1971, p.141.

18   Slater, P., Parental Role Differentiation, in Coser, R.L. (ed.) 'The Family, its Function and Structure', 2nd ed., Macmillan, London, 1974, pp.259-75.

19   Holman, R., The Place of Foster Care, 'British Journal of Social Work', spring 1975, vol. 5, no. 1, pp.3-29.

20   Rutter, M., op.cit., p.124.

21   George, V., 'Foster Care: Theory and Practice'. Routledge & Kegan Paul, London, 1970, pp.42-80.

22   Goldstein, J., Freud, A., Solneit, A.J., op.cit.

23   Ibid.

24   Young, M. and Willmott, P., 'Family and Kinship in East London', Routledge & Kegan Paul, London, 1957; Bott, E., 'Family and Social Network', Tavistock Publications, London, 1957; Freed, A.O., The Family Agency and the Kinship System, in 'Social Casework', December 1975, p.579-86. Litwak, E., Extended Kin Relations in an Industrial Society, in 'Social Structure and the Family', Shanes, E., and Streib, G. (eds), Prentice Hall, Englewood Cliffs, N.J., 1965, pp.290-323

25   Jenkins, S. and Norman, E., 'Filial Deprivation and Foster Care', Columbia University Press, New York and London 1972, and Oakley, R., Self Image and the Release of Children for Adoption, in 'Child Adoption', nos 2 and 3, 1974, pp.27-35.

26   Gough, K., The Origins of the Family, in 'The Journal of Marriage', vol. 33, no. 5, November, 1971, pp.760-71.

27   Freud, A., Children Possessed, 'Child Adoption', no. 3, 1975, pp.39-42.

28   Mannoni, M., 'The Child, His "Illness" and the Others', Tavistock Publications, London, 1970, p.ix. Quoted in Mitchell, J., (1975), op.cit., p.392.

29   Balint, E., Fair Shares and Mutual Concern (based on notes by Dr Michael Balint), 'International Journal of Psychoanalysis', vol. 53, no. 61, 1972, p.64.

30   Ibid., p.62.

31   Brailsford, H.N., 'The Levellers and the English Revolution', Cresset Press, London, 1961, ch. xxxiv; Coser, L.A., The Sexual Requisites of Utopia, in Coser, R.L. (ed.), op.cit., 2nd edn, 1974, pp.532-40; and Kanter, R.M., Oneida, Community of the Past, in Coser, R.L. (ed.), ibid., pp.541-9, are a few of many records of collective living.

32   Erikson, E., 'Identity: Youth and Crisis', Norton, New York, 1968, p.224.

33   Reich, R., op.cit., p.153.
34   Mills, R., 'Young Outsiders', Institute of Community Studies and
      Routledge & Kegan Paul, London, 1973, pp.176-8. See also Coser, L.A.,
      The Sexual Requisites of Utopia, in Coser, R.L. (ed.), op.cit., pp.532-40.
      2nd edn, 1974.
35   Ibid. and Speck, V., 'The New Families: Youth, Communes and the
      Politics of Drugs', Tavistock Publications, London, 1972.
36   Cooper, D., 'Death of the Family', op.cit., and Cooper, D., 'Grammar of
      Living', op.cit.
37   Speck, R.V., op.cit., p.19, and Rigby, A., 'Communes in Britain',
      Routledge & Kegan Paul, London, 1974, ch. 2.
38   Cooper, D., 'Death of the Family', op.cit., p.80.
39   Ibid.
40   Reich, R., op.cit., p.150.
41   Ibid., p.151.
42   Crowther, G., Self-sufficiency, Rural Commune – Special Offer,
      Bitbetter, London, no. 13, 1975.
43   Rigby, A., op.cit., p.58.
44   Kommune 2, 'Children and Political Collectives', Rising Free offprint,
      London, 1975.
45   E.g. A Lot More Messing About at the Edges, 'Spare Rib', no. 35,
      May 1975; 'Shrew' (Womens Liberation Workshop, London), vol. 4,
      no. 3, May 1971; Hann, J., 'But What About the Children', Bodley Head,
      London, 1976, ch. 5.
46   Rigby, A., op.cit., ch. 2.
47   Cooper, D., 'Grammar of Living', op.cit., p.86.
48   Kommune 2, op.cit., p.5.

Chapter 5 Biological destiny or the mind-forged manacles

1   Seecombe, W., The Housewife and Her Labour Under Capitalism, 'Red
     Rag' Pamphlet no. 3, IMG Publications, 182 Pentonville Rd, London N.1.,
     no date, p.19.
2   Firth, R., Review Symposium of Oakley, A., 'The Sociology of Housework',
     Martin Robertson, London, 1971, in 'Sociology', vol. 19, no. 3, September
     1975.
3   Wallman, S., Difference, Differentiation, Discrimination, in 'New
     Communities', vol. 5, no. 1-2, summer 1976, p.12.
4   Waller, K., A Study of Social Worker Attitudes to Women Clients
     Concentrating on Women in Families. Part 1. A survey of literature used
     on social work courses. Current Researcher, Leicester University, School
     of Social Work.
5   Oakley, A., 'Housewife', Allen Lane, London, 1974, and Rowbotham, S.,
     'Hidden from History', Pluto Press, London, 1973.
6   Hartnett, O., and Rendel, M., compiled by, 'Women's Studies in the UK,
     London Seminars', 71 Clifton Hill, London NW8 0JN, no date,
     pp 3-4.
7   Atkinson, D., 'Orthodox Consensus and Radical Alternatives', Heinemann,
     London, 1972 pp.183-8.
8   Benedek, T., (1956), quoted in Blos, P., 'Adolescence', Free Press, New
     York, 1962, p.144.
9   Bettleheim, B., The Commitment Required of a Woman Entering a

Scientific Profession in Present-day American Society. 'Women in the Scientific Professions', the MIT Symposium on American Women in Science and Engineering, 1965, quoted in Weisstein, N., Psychology Constructs the Female: or the Fantasy Life of the Male Psychologists, in 'Radical Therapist', Brown, P. (ed.), Tavistock Publications, London, 1973, p.391.

10   Rheingold, J., 'The Fear of Being Woman', Grune & Stratton, New York, 1964, quoted in Weisstein, N., op.cit., p.32.

11   Bouverman, D., Bouverman, I. and Clarkson, F., Sex Role Characteristics and Clinical Judgements of Mental Health, 'Journal of Consulting and Clinical Psychology', no. 34, 1970, and, by the same authors, Sex Role Stereotypes: a current appraisal, 'Journal of Social Issues', no.28, 1972, and Rozen Brown, C., Levit Hellinger, M., Therapists' Attitudes to Women, 'Social Work', Vol. 20, no. 4, July 1975, p.266.

12   Parker, N., A Psychiatrist's Viewpoint of Women's liberation, in McConaghy, N., (ed.), 'Liberation Movements and Psychiatry'; Ciba-Geigy, Australia Ltd, New South Wales, 1973, p.63.

13   Brown, G.W., Bhrolchain Maire Ni andHarris, T. Social Class and Psychiatric Disturbance Among Women in an Urban Population, 'Sociology', vol. 9, no. 2, May 1975, pp.225—45.

14   Atkinson, D., op.cit.

15   Oakley, A., 'Sex, Gender and Society', Maurice Temple Smith, London, 1972, and Hutt, C., 'Males and Females', Penguin, Harmondsworth, 1972.

16   See Breen, D., 'The Birth of the First Child', Tavistock Publications, London, 1975, pp.144-5.

17   Jones, I.H., Biological Limitations of the Women's Liberation Movement, in McConaghy, N., (ed.), op.cit., p.42.

18   Ibid.

19   Mitchell, J., 'Psychoanalysis and Feminism', Penguin, Harmondsworth, 1975, p.414.

20   Tiger, L., Male Dominance? Yes. Sexist Plot? No., 'New York Times Magazine', section N, 25 October 1970, referred to by Weisstein, N., op.cit., p.409.

21   Mitchell, G.D., Paternalistic Behaviour in Primates, 'Psychological Bulletin' 71, 1969, p.399-417, referred to in Weisstein, N., op.cit.

22   Weisstein, N., op.cit., p.410.

23   Ibid., p.413, and Morgan, P., 'Child Care Sense and Fable', Maurice Temple Smith, London, 1975, p.249-50.

24   Weisstein, N., op.cit., p.413

25   Comfort, A., 'Sex in Society', Penguin, Harmondsworth 1964, footnote to p.131.

26   Comfort, A., Sexuality in a Zero Growth Society, in Francoeur, R. and A. (eds), 'The Future of Sexual Relations', Spectrum, New Jersey, 1974, p.52-3.

27   Francoeur, R., The Technologies of Man-made Sex, in Francoeur, R. and A. (eds), op.cit., p.9.

28   Titmuss, R., 'Essays on the Welfare State', Allen & Unwin, London, 1958.

29   Kinsey, A.C., Pomeroy, W.B. and Martin, C.C., 'Sexual Behaviour in the Human Male', 1948, and Kinsey, A.C., Pomeroy, W.B., Martin, C.C. and Gebhard, P.H., 'Sexual Behaviour in the Human Female', 1953, both published by W.B. Saunders & Co., Philadelphia and London. Masters, W.H. and Johnson, V.E., 'Human Sexual Response', Little Brown,

Boston, 1966. For a discussion see Sherfey, M.J., On the Nature of Female Sexuality, in Miller, J.B., (ed.), 'Psychoanalysis and Women', Penguin, Harmondsworth, 1974, pp.136-53, and Oakley, A., (1972), op.cit.

30 Koedt, A., The Myth of the Vaginal Orgasm, in Brown, P., (ed.), op.cit. pp.133-41.

31 Ibid., p.102.

32 Ibid., p.142.

33 Radical Lesbians, Woman Identified Woman, in Brown, P., (ed.), op.cit., pp.472-3.

34 Cass, B., Testosterone — The Basis of Social Power or the Politics of Biological Determinism? in McConaghy, N., (ed.), op.cit., p.66.

35 Oakley, A., (1972), op.cit.

36 Herbert, J., The Development of Sexual Behaviour, 'New Society', vol. 16, no. 423, 5 November 1970, p.820.

37 Fletcher, R., Animal Adaptation, 'The Times Educational Supplement', 29 August 1975, (a review of Thorpe, V.H., 'Animal Nature and Human Nature', Methuen, London, 1975).

38 Waller, K., op.cit.

39 Most of this section is drawn from this book, and it is hoped will lead the reader to it.

40 Mitchell, J., (1975), op.cit., p.362.

41 Millet, K., 'Sexual Politics', Abacus edn, Sphere Books, London, 1972.

42 Mitchell, J., (1975), op.cit., See also Kupers T., Synthesis or Science, in 'Radical Psychology' in Brown, P., (ed.), Tavistock, London, 1973. For an opposite view see Millett, K., op.cit., Greer, G., 'The Female Eunuch', Paladin edn, London, 1971, and Brooks, K., Freudianism is Not a Basis for a Marxist Psychology, in Brown, P., (ed.), 'Radical Psychology', op.cit.

43 See Mitchell, J., (1975), op.cit., for the analysis.

44 Mannoni, O., 'Freud', Pantheon, New York, 1975, p.336.

45 Freud, S., 'An Outline of Psychoanalysis', standard edition, vol. XXIII, quoted in Mitchell, J., Female Sexuality, in 'Journal of Biosocial Science', no. 4, 1973, p.123-36.

46 In Mitchell, J., (1975), op.cit., p.50.

47 Raynor, E., 'Human Development', Allen & Unwin, London, 1971, p.51.

48 Ibid., p.154.

49 Other sources are 'Counselling Homosexuals', compiled by Peter Righton, Bedford Square Press, National Council of Social Service, 26 Bedford Square, London WC1, 1973, and Gay Liberation Front, 5 Caledonian Rd, London N1, for booklists.

50 Mitchell, J., (1975), p.53.

51 Ibid., p.28.

52 See 'Forum Magazine'.

53 Mitchell, J., (1975), p.69.

54 Quoted in ibid., p.11.

55 Socarides, quoted in West, D.J., Aspects of Homosexuality, in Harrison, G.A. and Peel, J., (eds), 'Biosocial Aspects of Sex', 'Journal of Biosocial Science', Supplement no. 2, May 1970, pp.44-5.

56 For a discussion see Mitchell, J., (1975), pp.121-31.

57 Winnicott, D.W., The Split-off Male and Female Element to be Found in Men and Women, in 'Playing and Reality', Tavistock Publications, London, 1971, p.76 footnote.

58   Ibid., p.79.
59   Ibid., p.78.
60   Brown, P., (ed.), 'Radical Therapist', op.cit., chs 16 and 17, and Rice,
      J.K. and Rice, D.G., Implications of the Women's Liberation Movement
      for Psychotherapy, 'American Journal of Psychiatry', vol. 130, no. 2,
      February 1973, pp.191-6.
61   Mannoni, O., in Mitchell, J., (1975), p.336.
62   Rice, J.K., and Rice, D.G., op.cit., and Rozen Brown, C., Levit
      Hellinger, M., op.cit.
63   Oakley, A., (1972), op.cit., p.16.
64   Sears, R., Maccoby, E. and Levin, H., 'Patterns of Child-rearing',
      Harper, New York, 1957.
65   Oakley, A., (1972), op.cit., ch. 6.
66   Stoller, R.J., The 'Bedrock' of Masculinity and Femininity, in Baker,
      J.M., (ed.), op.cit., p.283.
67   Louie, E., The Trans-sexual Metamorphosis, in Francoeur, R. and A., (eds),
      op.cit., pp.122-8.
68   Oakley, A., (1972), op.cit.
      See also Firth, R., Review symposium, op.cit., pp.515-18 on symbolic
      perceptions of sex.
69   Quoted in Rowbotham, S., op.cit., p.6.
70   Watt, I., The New Woman in Samuel Richardson's 'Pamela', in Coser,
      R.L., (ed.), 'The Family, Its Functions and Structure', 1st edition, St.
      Martins Press, New York, 1964.
71   Callahan, S., The Future of the Sexually Liberated Woman, in Francoeur,
      R. and A., (eds), op.cit., p.107-11.
72   Milligan, D., Homosexuality, Sexual Needs and Problems, in Bailey, R. and
      M., (eds), 'Radical Social Work', Edward Arnold, London, 1975.
      pp.96-111.
73   Members of the Armed Forces, the Merchant Navy, Scotland, and
      under-18-year-olds are excluded from the Acts' provision.
74   Kinsey, A.C., et al., 'Sexual Behaviour in the Human Male', Kinsey et al.,
      'Sexual Behaviour in the Human Female', op.cit.
75   Firth, R., The Social Images of Man and Woman, in Harrison, G.A., and
      Peel, J., (eds), Journal of Social Sciences Supplementary, 'Biosocial
      Aspects of Sex', Proceedings of the Annual Symposium of Eugenics
      Society, London, 1969, Blackwell, Oxford, 1970, pp.87-90.
76   Dahrendorf, R., 'Homo Sociologicus', Routledge & Kegan Paul, London,
      1973, pp.3-4.
77   Emmet, D., 'Roles, Rules and Relations', Macmillan, London, 1966,
      p.140.
78   Atkinson, D., op.cit., p.157.
79   Banton, M., 'Roles', Tavistock, London, 1975, p.36.
80   Gross, N., Mason, W. and McEachern, A., 'Explorations in Role Analysis',
      Wiley, New York, 1958.
81   See Atkinson, D., op.cit., ch. 6, for a discussion.
82   Ibid., pp.158-64.
83   Ibid, ch. 6.
84   Ibid., p.150.
85   Schumpeter, J.A., 'Capitalism, Socialism and Democracy', Allen & Unwin,
      London, 4th edn, 1943, p.82.
86   Koramovsky, M., Cultural Contradiction and Sex Roles, in Coser, R.L.,
      (ed.), 'The Family, Its Functions and Structure', 2nd edn, Macmillan.

London, 1974. p.512.
87 Firth, op.cit., Oakley, A., (1972), op.cit., Coser, R.L., (ed.), op.cit., 2nd edn.
88 Race Relations Acts, 1965, 1968 and Race Relations Act 1976, Sex Discrimination Act, 1975, and Sexual Offences Act, 1967.
89 Dahrendorf, R., op.cit., p.22.
90 Emmet, D., op.cit., p.173.
91 Banton, M., op.cit., p.36.
92 Dahrendorf, R., op.cit., p.32.
93 Report of the Committee on One-parent Families (Finer Report), HMSO, London, Cmnd 5629-1, vol. 1, paras 8.125 and 8.128 (4).
94 Banton, R., op.cit., p.139., Emmet, D., op.cit., p.15., Dahrendorf, R., op.cit., p.84.
95 Merton, R.K., 'Social Theory and Social Structure', Free Press, New York, 1968, pp.425ff.
96 Epstein, C.F., Reconciliation of Women's Roles, in Coser, R.L., (ed.), (1974), op.cit., 2nd edn, pp.480ff.
97 Community Relations Commission, 'Who minds? A Study of Working Mothers and Child-minding in Ethnic Minority Communities, Reference and Technical Devision', 15-16 Bedford Square, London WC2E 9HX, July 1975.
98 Mothers in Action, 'Opportunities for School-age Children', Mothers in Action, London, November 1974.
99 Weber, M., referred to in Coser, R.L. and Rokoff, G., Women in the Occupational World: Social Disruption and Conflict, in Coser R.L., (1974), op.cit., 2nd edn, p.491.
100 'Womanpower: Study Group', 'Young Fabian Pamphlet', No. 11, 1966, p.23.
101 Coser, R.L. and Rokoff, G., in Coser, R.L., (ed.), (1974), op.cit., pp.490-511.
102 George, V. and Wilding, P., 'Motherless Families', Routledge & Kegan Paul, London, 1972.
103 Some absences for men from work are being legitimated, e.g. paternity leave during birth of baby, particularly the second child or, more exceptionally, agreements that 'maternity leave' can be taken either by the mother or by the father of the child where both are employed in the same university.
104 Sharpe, S., The Role of the Nuclear Family in the Oppression of Women, in 'The Body Politic: Women's Liberation in Britain, 1969-72', Stage 1, 21 Theobalds Rd, London, 1972, p.139.
105 Dicks, H., 'Marital Tensions', Routledge & Kegan Paul, London, 1967, p.33. See for a discussion, Waller, K., op.cit.
106 Ackerman, N., 'Psychodynamics of Family Life', and 'Treating the Troubled Family', Basic Books, New York, 1966.
107 Waller, K., op.cit.
108 Larguia, L. and Dumoulin, J., 'Towards a Science of Women's Liberation', published as 'Red Rag' Pamphlet No. 1, no date, 9 Stratford Villas, London NW1.
109 Parsons, T., Age, Sex in the Social Structure, in Coser, R.L., (ed.), (1974), op.cit., 2nd edn, p.252.
110 Ibid., p.244.
112 Coser, R.L., (ed.), (1974), op.cit., 2nd edn, section 9.
112 Goldstein, J., Freud, A. and Solneit, A.J., 'Beyond the Best Interests of

the Child', Collier Macmillan, London, 1973.

113   Holman, R., The Place of Foster Care, 'British Journal of Social Work', vol. 5, no. 1, Spring 1975, pp.3-29.

114   Heilbrun, C.G., Recognising the Androgynous Human, in Francoeur, R. and A., (eds), op.cit.

115   McLuhan, M. and Leonard, E.B., The Future of Sex, in Francoeur, R. and A., (eds), op.cit., O'Neill, N. and O'Neill, G., 'Open Marriage', Lippincott, New York, 1972; Francoeur, A.K. and K., Francoeur, R.T., Hot and Cool Sex – Closed and Open Marriages, in Francoeur, R. and A., (eds), op.cit.

116   Francoeur, R. and A., (eds), op.cit., p.35.

117   McLuhan, M. and Leonard, E.B., op.cit.

118   Leonard, G.B., Why We Need a New Sexuality, in Francoeur, R. and A., (eds), op.cit., pp.26-9.

119   McLuhan, M. and Leonard, E.B., op.cit.

120   Ibid.

121   Comfort, A., Sexuality in a Zero Growth Society, in Francoeur, R. and A., (eds), op.cit.

122   Mitchell, J., (1975), op.cit.; Millett, K., op.cit.

123   Lévi-Strauss, C., 'Structural Anthropology', Allen Lane, London, 1968.

124   For a discussion see Mitchell, J., (1975), pp.370-6.

125   Ibid., p.409. In March 1976 NCCL proposed the abolition of incest as a crime.

126   Larguia, L. and Dumoulin, J., op.cit., p.13.

127   Mitchell, J., (1975), p.408.

Chapter 6 Towards a conclusion

1   Miliband, R., 'The State in a Capitalist Society', Weidenfeld & Nicolson, London, 1969, ch. 9.

2   E.g. Report of the Committee on One-parent Families (Finer Report), Cmnd 5629-1, and recommendations for One-parent Family and Chronically Sick and Disabled Persons Act, 1970.

3   Yelloly, M.A., Professional Ideology in British Social Work with Particular Reference to the Influence of Psychoanalysis, Ph.D. thesis, University of Leicester, 1975.

4   Leonard, P., Poverty, Consciousness and Action. The Sheila Kay Memorial Lecture, April 1975, p.9 of stencilled copy.

5   Miliband, R., op.cit., ch. 9.

6   Ibid., and Alfrero, A.L. Conscientisation, in 'New Themes in Social Work Education', International Schools of Social Work, 1972. Proceedings of XVI International Congress of Schools of Social Work, p.80.

7   Cohen, S., It's All Right For You to Talk. Political and Sociological Manifestos, in Bailey, R. and Brake, M., (eds), 'Radical Social Work', Edward Arnold, London, 1975, pp.92-5.

8   Miliband, R., op.cit., p.267.

9   Ander Egg, E., 'El Servicio en la Encrucija', Mexico City, Mexico ed Fownier, 1971, quoted in Alfrero, L.A., op.cit., p.81.

10   Leonard, P., op.cit., p.8.

11   For an opposite point of view see Brown, P., 'Red Radical Therapist', Tavistock, London, 1973.

12   Leonard, P., op.cit., p.8.

13 Alfrero, A.L., op.cit.
14 Alfrero, A.L., op.cit., p.80.
15 Ibid., p.72.
16 Bronfenbrenner, U., 'Two Worlds of Childhood, US and USSR', Russell Sage Foundation, New York, and Allen & Unwin, London, 1971; and Erikson, E., 'Childhood and Society', Horton, New York, 1950.
17 Towle, C., 'Common Human Needs', National Association of Social Workers, New York, 1965.
18 Rutter, M., 'Maternal Deprivation, Reassessed', Penguin, Harmondsworth, 1972.
19 See Thompson, E.P., 'The Making of the English Working Class', Gollancz, London, 1964.
20 Education Group, Gay Social Workers and Probation Officers.
21 'Boarding Out of Children Regulations 1955', Statutory Instruments no. 1377, s. 2, HMSO, London.

Select bibliography

Atkinson, D., 'Orthodox Consensus and Radical Alternatives', Heinemann, London, 1972.

Alfrero, L.A., Conscientisation, in 'New Themes in Social Work Education', International Schools of Social Work, 1972. Proceedings of XVI International Congress of Schools of Social Work.

Bailey, R. and Brake, M. (eds), 'Radical Social Work', Edward Arnold, London, 1975.

Balint, E., Fair Shares and Mutual Concern, 'International Journal of Psychoanalysis', 1972.

Bottomore, T.B. and Rubel, M., 'Karl Marx, Selected Writings in Sociology and Social Philosophy', Penguin, Harmondsworth, 1961.

Bronfenbrenner, U., 'Two Worlds of Childhood, USA and USSR', Russell Sage Foundation, New York; Allen & Unwin, London, 1971.

Cooper, D., 'Dialectics of Liberation', Penguin, Harmondsworth, 1968.

Cooper, D., 'Death of the Family', Allen Lane, London, 1971.

Cooper, D., 'Grammar of Living', Allen Lane, London, 1974.

Coser, R.L. (ed.), 'The Family, Its Functions and Structure', St Martin's Press, New York, 1st edn 1964; 2nd edn, Macmillan, London, 1974.

Francoeur, R. and A. (eds), 'The Future of Sexual Relations', Spectrum, New Jersey, 1974.

Friere, P., 'Pedagogy of the Oppressed', Penguin, Harmondsworth, 1972.

Goodman, J.A. (ed.), 'The Dynamics of Racism in Social Work Practice', NASW, Washington, 1973.

Illich, I., 'Celebration of Awareness', Penguin, Harmondsworth, 1973.

Kommune 2, 'Children in Political Collectives', offprint from Rising Free, London, 1975.

Larguia, I. and Dumoulin, J., 'Towards a Science of Women's Liberation', 'Red Rag' Pamphlet no. 1, 9 Stratford Villas, London NW1.

Lipman, B.J., The Implications for Family Structure of Changing Sex Roles, 'Social Casework', February 1976, pp.67-79.

McDermott, F.E., 'Self-Determination in Social Work', Routledge & Kegan

Paul, London, 1975.

Marcuse, H., 'Eros and Civilisation', Abacus edn, Sphere Books, London, 1972.

Marcuse, H., 'One Dimensional Man', Abacus edn, Sphere Books, London, 1972.

Miliband, R., 'The State in Capitalist Society', Weidenfeld & Nicolson, London, 1969

Miller Baker, Joan, 'Psychoanalysis and Women', Penguin, Harmondsworth, 1973.

Mishra, R., Marx and Welfare, 'Sociological Review', vol.23, no.2, new series, pp.287-313.

Mitchell, J., 'Women's Estate', Penguin, Harmondsworth, 1971.

Mitchell, J., 'Psychoanalysis and Feminism', Penguin, Harmondsworth, 1975.

Oakley, A., 'Sex, Gender and Society', Temple Smith, London, 1972.

Otto, H.A., 'The Family in Search of a Future', Appleton Century Crofts, New York, 1970.

Parkin, F., 'Class Inequality and the Political Order', Paladin, London, 1971.

Reich, R., 'Sexuality and the Class Struggle', Praeger, New York, 1971.

Resnick, R.P., Conscientisation: An Indigenous Approach to International Social Work, 'International Social Work', vol. XIX, no. 1, 1976.

Roszak, T., 'The Making of a Counter Culture', Faber & Faber, London, 1970.

Ryan, W., 'Blaming the Victim', Vintage Books, New York, 1972.

Stein, H., Eileen Younghusband Lecture, November 1970 (unpublished).

Wilson, L., 'Women and the Welfare State', 'Red Rag' Pamphlet no. 2, 9 Stratford Villas, London NW1.

Winnicott, D.W., The Split-off Male and Female Element to be Found in Men and Women, in 'Playing and Reality', Tavistock, London, 1971.

Index

118

Index